MW00365696

"This is NOT a book about 'being nice.' It is an in-depth, practical, and inspiring guide that explores the challenges and rewards of BEING loving and kind in our daily lives."

— DON EATON, singer-songwriter, recording artist, and inspirational speaker

"I really appreciated this book and plan to use it with my congregation. I want to be more compassionate, forgiving, and generous, but too often fall short. This book drew me in and helped me reflect on these things that I wish for in my journey to be more compassionate. I found that I didn't just have to wish, but began choosing lovingkindness in tangible ways. Bill Miller makes lovingkindness accessible and offers us questions and reflections to help us embrace the love that is already in us. This is a book to be savored!"

— SUE JOINER, senior minister, First Congregational United Church of Christ, Albuquerque, NM

Lovingkindness

Lovingkindness

Realizing and Practicing Your True Self

WILLIAM R. MILLER

 CASCADE *Books* · Eugene, Oregon

LOVINGKINDNESS
Realizing and Practicing Your True Self

Copyright © 2017 William R. Miller. All rights reserved. Except for brief quotations in critical publications or reviews, no part of this book may be reproduced in any manner without prior written permission from the publisher. Write: Permissions, Wipf and Stock Publishers, 199 W. 8th Ave., Suite 3, Eugene, OR 97401.

Cascade Books
An Imprint of Wipf and Stock Publishers
199 W. 8th Ave., Suite 3
Eugene, OR 97401

www.wipfandstock.com

PAPERBACK ISBN: 978-1-4982-9839-1
HARDCOVER ISBN: 978-1-4982-4889-1
EBOOK ISBN: 978-1-4982-9840-7

Cataloguing-in-Publication data:

Names: Miller, William R.
Title: Lovingkindness : realizing and practicing your true self / William R. Miller.
Description: Eugene, OR: Cascade Books, 2017.
Identifiers: ISBN 978-1-4982-9839-1 (paperback) | ISBN 978-1-4982-4889-1 (hardcover) | ISBN 978-1-4982-9840-7 (ebook)
Subjects: LCSH: Love. | Kindness. | Title.
Classification: BF575.L8 M38 2017 (print) | BF575.L8 (ebook)

Manufactured in the U.S.A.   MAY 22, 2017

Biblical quotations are from the New Revised Standard Version Bible, copyright 1989, Division of Christian Education of the National Council of the Churches of Christ in the United States of America. Used by permission. All rights reserved.

In memory of Carl R. Rogers, PhD

Love is patient; love is kind; love is not envious or boastful or arrogant or rude. It does not insist on its own way; it is not irritable or resentful; it does not rejoice in wrong-doing, but rejoices in the truth. It bears all things, believes all things, hopes all things, endures all things. Love never ends.

1 COR 13:4–8A

Table of Contents

Preface

The world can surely seem a dark place at times. In every age that has left a language record there have been periods and places of horrific evil, far too many to enumerate. The evening news offers a constant drone of human inhumanity and this is surely nothing new.

Yet even a small point of light disperses darkness. The most potent response to inhumanity is to live against it, to respond not in kind but in true opposition. The opposite of inhumanity is not passivity. It is lovingkindness.

To live consistently in a loving and kind way is challenging enough with those whom we know and love, but the age-old calling is higher still: to extend lovingkindness to strangers and even to those who hold enmity toward us, who have harmed us or would seek to do so. The greater the harm, the greater is the challenge. How, for example, can one possibly respond to violence with compassion when it is so human to cry out for vengeance? Yet that is precisely what we have been challenged to do by the Buddha, Gandhi, Martin Luther King Jr., Jesus, Muhammad, Mother Teresa, Elie Wiesel, and countless other men and women deeply rooted in spirituality.

If there is a point on which world religions converge, it is in calling humankind to practice compassion. Lovingkindness is not what we *have* to do in all our affairs, and it surely is not always what we *want* to do, but it is something that we *can* do. It is possible, a choice that we can make in any circumstance. It is within our ken and grasp to do so, and in a larger moral sense it is what we *must* do for the human family to survive and mature.

This book explores the promise and challenge of living with lovingkindness, a concept with deep ancient roots. What exactly is it in practice? How can we more fully and consistently live this calling to be a loving presence in the world? How does doing so affect us and those around us? The answers are at once both simple and elusive.

In truth, lovingkindness is not something that we can achieve or perfect. It is more like a star by which to guide our life journey, a distant goal toward or away from which we move along the way in the countless choices that we make each day. This book is about that journey.

1

The Calling

They were as different from each other as Americans could be. They ranged in age across four generations representing a wide span of occupations, ethnicity, income, and lifestyle. In fact, there was only one thing that they all had in common. All of them had had a remarkable and highly memorable experience that changed them forever.

These women and men participated in what was for me the most fascinating and rewarding study of my forty-year career in psychological research. I set out to discover whether overnight personality transformations—the kind popularized in Charles Dickens's beloved story of Ebenezer Scrooge—actually occur in real life. Such experiences appear in biography and autobiography, in the life stories of people as diverse as Jane Addams and Malcolm X, Fyodor Dostoevsky and Simone Weil, Bill Wilson and the Buddha. Do such transformations really happen to ordinary people?

As it turned out it was not difficult to find them. A single story in the Sunday *Albuquerque Journal* set the telephone ringing for weeks. It described the phenomenon as a sudden, unexpected, highly memorable experience lasting for a few minutes or hours that leaves the person permanently and profoundly changed. Altogether, eighty-nine people responded to that one story, of whom fifty-five volunteered three hours of their time to describe their experience and answer some standard questions. They were fascinated to learn that such experiences had happened to other people, and though most had divulged it to no one or very few people, they were eager to tell us their story.

The study left me with a clear conviction that such "quantum changes" are real, that they do happen to ordinary as well as extraordinary people, and in fact are not all that rare.[1] The experiences were relatively brief and completely unexpected. No one was trying to have such an experience and none thought it was something that they had done or accomplished themselves. Instead, they were grateful recipients, and their "why me?" question reflected their wonderment as to the reasons why they, of all people, were so privileged to have such an experience.

It was one particular aspect of these stories that planted in me the seed for this book. About half of the people we interviewed had experienced what we called a *mystical* type of quantum change. They had brief and intense awe-inspiring experiences, often with a sense of transcending time and space. Most felt themselves in the presence of some Other far greater than themselves that they never saw but definitely experienced. Some had no prior concept or name for this experience, nothing to which they could relate it. Those with a religious history tended to identify the Other in the language of their own faith. All had great difficulty putting their experience into words. It defied language. What struck me in studying the interviews was that no matter the person's background, their particular religion or none, male or female, young or old, rich or poor, these people who had never met each other seemed to be describing the same Other. It was as if they had encountered the same presence, although they drew on different names and metaphors to describe it.

And it surprised them. Even those with a Judeo-Christian background did not encounter the stereotypical God of Western culture. They were not afraid. They knew certainly that they were in the presence of something infinitely greater than themselves, something of vast power, but they were not terrified. Quite to the contrary, what they felt and described was an experience of being totally, absolutely, completely loved and accepted. They knew and felt it to their very depths and it changed them. It was an acceptance and love beyond their comprehension that could not be adequately recounted in words, and in a sense there was no need for them to describe or understand it. They simply knew it for certain and realized in that moment that they would never be the same again. They had passed through a one-way door. Some were released from pain, addiction, or burdens of fear and anger. Some embarked on a completely new path while others continued on their prior journey with a new vision and vibrancy. What they all seemed to share was the sure knowledge that the nature of that Other, whoever or whatever it may be, was a profound, inexpressible, unconditional, and utterly accepting love. This mystical experience was well described by Paul Tillich in 1948.

> It is as though a voice were saying: "You are accepted. You are accepted, accepted by that which is greater than you, and the name of which you do not know. Do not ask for the name now; perhaps you will find it later. Do not try to do anything now; perhaps later you will do much. Do not seek for anything; do not intend anything. Simply accept the fact that you are accepted." [2]

Among the changes that these people experienced immediately and in the decades that followed was a sense of utter safety.[3] Not that they were free from the pain, problems, and challenges of life—not at all, but they knew that whatever may come they were in the deepest sense safe and secure. They also seemed to have no need to persuade others of the truth of what they had experienced. They did not proselytize. They knew.

A number of them also had a further insight: that the profound love they had experienced in the Other is also our essential nature as humans. It is what we *are*, and at the same time what we are meant to be. We do have a choice about it, but this is the inherent blueprint toward which we grow. This lovingkindness in us is like the oak tree hidden within the acorn. It will emerge if given the right conditions, and when we are growing in that direction we are becoming what it is that we are naturally meant to be. In that moment of insight they experienced an intimate connected-ness with all other humans, with all of life, or even with the entire universe. It is not that we are all in the same boat, but that we *are* the same boat, made of the same essence that is in all humankind and in the Other.

Pretty mystical stuff! Most of them had never talked to anyone about what they saw and experienced. Often, their story sounded rather crazy and they weren't sure that anyone else could understand, but then our article appeared in the newspaper indi-cating that perhaps others had had experiences like theirs and they wanted to tell their story.

Are they right? Is lovingkindness truly in our very nature, that which we are naturally meant to be? Do we have in our DNA the likeness of this great Other whose name we may not even know? The writer C. S. Lewis believed that there are certain humane values that we innately share as human beings, qualities that we recognize and honor when we encounter them—if not universally, at least widely.[4] In "Charter for Compassion," Karen Armstrong similarly affirmed that

> the principle of compassion lies at the heart of all reli-gious, ethical and spiritual traditions, calling us always to treat all others as we wish to be treated ourselves. Compassion impels us to work tirelessly to alleviate the suffering of our fellow creatures, to dethrone ourselves from the center of our world and put another there, and to honor the inviolable sanctity of every single human being, treating everybody, without exception, with abso-lute justice, equity and respect.[5]

Lovingkindness is our original blueprint, the very best in us. It is not our only possible nature and future, of course, as individu-als or as a species. We have a say in the matter, a choice about who and how we will be. Yet there is something about lovingkindness that calls to us, and when we experience or practice it there is a feeling of homecoming, of being where we belong. I hope that this book will help you realize and live out that intention.

2

The Nature of Human Nature

So what is our basic nature as human beings? There are at least three different views that have emerged over the centuries. Call them simply Theory A, B, and C.

Three Perspectives on Human Nature

Theory A

One view is that at our core, human beings are corrupt and self-centered—that what is deep inside when all the layers are finally stripped away is a dark mass of violent and self-serving instincts. Within the discipline of psychology this view is associated with Sigmund Freud who conceptualized the unconscious mind as primitive human impulses. Left to our own devices without laws and social control we would quickly degenerate into the destructive self-absorption depicted in William Golding's classic novel, *Lord of the Flies.*

Theory A is continually reinforced by what is usually offered as news in public media. On a day when there is insufficient cruelty in our own community, newscasters bring us stories of appalling inhumanity from other places. The impression of one's community and of human nature more generally that is selectively promulgated by news coverage is unmistakably Theory A. People should not be trusted.

Theory B

Theory B is that there really is no characteristic essential human nature. We are simply the product of the genes that we happen to inherit interacting with and shaped by whatever experiences we chance to encounter along the way. This is now a dominant perspective within academic psychology, that everything we do is determined by heredity and environment. If one just knew enough about a person's biology and learning history it would be possible to predict (and perhaps even control) his or her actions, with a certain allowance for random chaos. Within Theory B, at the core of human nature we are a kind of blank slate written upon by the happenstance of nature and nurture. We have no inherent true self and we are in fact controlled by our unconscious wiring, much as a computer can only respond according to its programming and the information that it has received.

What these two popular views, Theory A and Theory B, have in common is the belief that what we do is actually predetermined, predictable. Choice and self-direction are mere illusions.[6]

Theory C

In response to these two views of human nature—psychoanalysis and behaviorism—there arose a third force within the history of psychology. Theory C embraces *choice* as a fundamental aspect of human nature. Within some limits of nature and nurture we decide what we do and who we are. Aware of it or not we are responsible for the choices that we make and thus for who we become. The psychiatrist Viktor Frankl, a Nazi concentration camp survivor, observed that what could never be taken away from human beings in the camps was this choice of how to be.[7]

Some thinkers within this third force have taken Theory C a step further, asserting and trusting the essential goodness of human nature. If undistorted, the natural direction of human development is toward positive growth and pro-social choices. Celtic spirituality similarly affirms the essential loving goodness of all creation, including humankind.[8] Within each person is a unique loving self, a fundamental nature that is either fostered or impeded by experience, and movement toward this essential nature is the realization of one's true self.[9]

In ancient Greek a term for the essential nature of a thing was its *telos*. The *telos* of an acorn, its fully matured and developed form, is an oak tree. The blueprint of the mature being, its intended nature, is already contained in the seed. In biblical usage, *telos* is sometimes translated as "perfect," as in the exhortation to "be perfect, even as God is perfect."[10] The connotation of "perfect" in English is to have no flaws, to make no mistakes, but *telos* is something quite different from that. It is the fully mature and developed form, flaws and all. The exhortation is to become our true self, that which we are meant and intended to be.

Which of these three theories of human nature do you choose to believe? One can mount logical arguments for or against any of them, and none can be proved true beyond a reasonable doubt. Ironically, the theory that one endorses comes down to a matter of choice, of faith.

It does matter, though, which view of human nature you embrace because basic assumptions have a way of coming true.[11] If you believe that others are essentially self-serving, untrustworthy, and inconsiderate then you naturally approach people in a cautious, suspicious, and self-protective manner. Doing this in turn inspires and evokes the same from others because suspicion and subterfuge are contagious and so the assumption is confirmed, a self-fulfilling prophecy. The expectation that people are generally loving, caring, and trustworthy also tends to be realized. To see others in a benevolent light tends to bring out the best in them. There will be exceptions to the rule, of course, but in general you get what in your heart you expect: what you see is what you get.

There is good reason to treat others as you yourself wish to be treated, and to see others as you wish to be seen!

Humanity, Inhumanity, and Neutrality

Now suppose that both aspects of Theory C were true: (1) that our *telos*—our fundamental, natural, intended, and mature nature—is lovingkindness; and (2) that we also have a choice in the matter; we get to decide how we will live and be in whatever time we have in this world. We all have within us the potential for lovingkindness, for humanity (our blueprint loving nature) or inhumanity (its opposite). We live out our lives with some chosen admixture of humanity, inhumanity, and neutrality.

Neutrality? Yes, there is a region in between humanity and inhumanity, but consider first the ends of this character dimension.

The *humane* end of the spectrum involves acting toward others in a loving and empathic manner that respects, values, and honors them as fellow members of the human family. To be humane is to act on behalf of the welfare and happiness of others, to treat them as you would wish to be treated yourself. In ideal form this lovingkindness asks for nothing in return, and its nature is considered in more depth in chapter 3.

The *inhumane* end of this continuum of being involves acting toward others with the effect or intent of harming or depriving them. This may be done for self-gain (as in theft or kidnapping), on behalf of some larger purpose (as in warfare or terrorism), or for the sheer perverse gratification of exercising power and inflicting harm (as in rape or torture). Most crime is a clear example of inhumane action, but not all forms of inhumanity are illegal. One's occupation, investments, or lifestyle may quite legally yield personal gain by actively contributing to the harm of others.

Both humanity and inhumanity involve chosen action. In between the two is the realm of neutrality or inaction, which is also a choice. If *empathy* is the motivation behind humane action and *antipathy* is a driving force behind inhumanity, then the mind-set behind neutral inaction is *apathy*, an absence of apparent feeling or concern for others. Greed involves indifference for others relative to one's own acquisition. The *de facto* hope in gambling is for financial gain at the expense of others. Apathy involves *doing nothing* on behalf of others. Sometimes fear underlies apathy, like a bystander who witnesses a victim suffering but does nothing to intervene out of concern for personal safety.

Major world religions converge in denouncing not only antipathy (do not murder or steal) but apathy as well—both the sins of commission (such as actively harming others) and of omission (failing to act on behalf of others).

> I was hungry and you gave me no food, I was thirsty and you gave me nothing to drink. I was a stranger and you did not welcome me, naked and you did not give me clothing, sick and in prison and you did not visit me.[12]

In the classic Dickens tale, *A Christmas Carol*, the ghost of Jacob Marley is tormented most by his inaction during life, the missed opportunities for humanity that should have been his "business."

> In life my spirit never roved beyond the narrow limits of our money-changing hole. . . . Mankind was my business. The common welfare was my business; charity, mercy, forbearance, and benevolence, were, all, my business. The dealings of my trade were but a drop of water in the comprehensive ocean of my business!

Indeed, Dickens depicted the more general torment of the restless spirits of the night when now witnessing human suffering, as remorse at what they had not done in life.

> The misery with them all was, clearly, that they sought to interfere, for good, in human matters, and had lost the power forever.

Scrooge's own celebrated transformation is from an occupation of greed and a life of apathy and antipathy to one of generosity and lovingkindness.

We have, then, these three gears in the transmission of our lives: forward, neutral, and reverse. Forward moves us ahead toward the horizon of our humanity, that which we are meant to be. Reverse moves us further away from our humane nature. Neutral leaves us immobile, drifting with the tides around us. To live in neutral is to neglect our mature nature and purpose, our *telos*. The Hindu belief in reincarnation is essentially that we continue being reborn until we finally get this right.

Every life journey is spent in some combination of these three gears. The challenge is to spend more of our time, talent, and resources in forward gear fulfilling our humanity while expending less in neutral or reverse. Loving is not an optional extra to fit in if and when we have time. It is our essence, our breath. To live with lovingkindness is not a one-time choice, although as discussed in chapter 1 some people do experience sudden Scrooge-like epiphanies. Rather, it is an ongoing journey, the continuous flow of intentional choices small and large. I hope to offer here a practical companion guide on that chosen journey toward a humane life of lovingkindness.

3

What Is Lovingkindness?

Ancient Roots

The concept of lovingkindness is truly ancient. In Hebrew scripture dating back three thousand years the word is *hesed*, which has been translated into English in various ways, sometimes as "steadfast love" or "grace." The term *lovingkindness* was introduced into the English language by Myles Coverdale as a rendering of *hesed* in his 1535 translation of the Bible. This same term has been applied to closely related concepts from Baha'i, Buddhism, Christianity, Hinduism, and Islam. In the Pāli canon of Buddhism it is *mettā*, an unattached or unconditional lovingkindness. I have intentionally retained the single run-on word (rather than two separate words: loving kindness) because it is neither just loving nor mere kindness but a merger of the two, of loving intention and kind action. As with a marriage, they are not merely coupled, hyphenated separates (loving-kindness) but also one.

A closely related term in ancient Greek is *kharis*, the root of the English word "charity" and also often translated as "grace." Aristotle used this word to describe a gift or favor that is given freely with no expectation of return (*kharisma*). Similarly, "If you do good to those who do good to you, what *kharis* is that to you? If you lend to those from whom you hope to receive, what *kharis* is that to you?"[13] In other words, giving in order to receive love, recognition, or favors in return is not *kharis*.

Another ancient Greek term *agape* is most often translated as "love," as in "love your neighbor as yourself"[14] and "love your enemies."[15] *Agape* shares with *kharis* and the older word *hesed* the important aspect that it is unearned. It is given solely because it is the right thing to do, not because it is deserved or for personal gain or love in return. In a first-century letter a*gape* is described as patient, kind (*kharis*), rejoicing in the truth, bearing and believing and hoping all things, and never ending.[16] In opposite terms within the same letter *agape* is not envious, boastful, arrogant, rude, irritable, resentful, or insistent on one's own way. Obviously, this is a high calling, a guiding but unreachable star to follow.

The Heart of Lovingkindness

Drawing on these ancient roots, lovingkindness seems to have at least five key characteristics.

1. It is *chosen*. Lovingkindness is a choice among possibilities. It is not done unwillingly or grudgingly. To respond with lovingkindness is an act of heart and will, a conscious and intentional choice among possible ways of being.

2. It is *enacted*. Lovingkindness is not a private experience or emotion, not just subjective sympathy but compassionate action. Until enacted it is only *potential* lovingkindness. It is actualized in the doing.

3. It is *empathic*. Lovingkindness sees the world through the other's eyes. This does not mean that you share or agree with others' views, only that you have a compassionate interest in understanding their perspective and dilemma. It is not about giving others what *you* need; lovingkindness is about understanding and doing what is needed for another's well-being, even at cost to yourself. Empathy displaces both *apathy* (the lack of feeling, concern, and action) and *antipathy* (feeling or acting against another).

4. It is *selfless*. Lovingkindness is not done for your own personal gain or reward. No repayment is expected or desired. Lovingkindness does not require or rely on gratitude or anything else that can be given in return. Rather, it is given *with* and *from* gratitude and empathy. The purest acts of lovingkindness may be those where no reciprocation is even possible. When you practice lovingkindness no one owes you anything, not even gratitude. Neither is it earned; lovingkindness is not given because a person deserves it. It is simply given even when it is undeserved. It is not limited to those for and from whom you feel affection, but ideally extends to all including strangers and even those who wish or would do you harm.

5. It is *consistent*. Finally, lovingkindness is not an isolated act, not an exception to the norm. It is a chosen way of being in all one's affairs. Lovingkindness is reliable, steadfast. It is not withheld for cause and thus conditional. It does not come and go, extended and withdrawn in response to changing circumstance or merit. Lovingkindness is meant to be our default condition. To make this a normal and consistent way of living is truly an act of heart and will, although with practice it does become more natural (as do the habits of apathy and antipathy).

This is a very high bar indeed if you aspire to perfection, to error-free performance, but lovingkindness is a *telos*, a fully mature end state toward which to grow. The acorn has a very long way to go to become a towering oak tree, and from the ground the task looks unimaginable. The good news is that lovingkindness is already hardwired in us. It is our inborn blueprint just as the image of the oak tree is implanted in the acorn. Unlike the acorn we do have a choice. In each day's countless forks in the road we can choose to act with lovingkindness or not. It is within our grasp, and the quantum changers described in chapter 1, who experienced firsthand a loving Other, knew that we do have a guiding star and are growing like heliotropes toward its light.

4

Practicing Lovingkindness:
Twelve Choices We Make

In a way the nature of lovingkindness is quite simple: to act for the well-being of others. It can be helpful, though, to step down from this lofty aspiration to more specific and practical expressions found in everyday life. Although lovingkindness can be shown in heroic sacrificial acts such as giving one's life for another, it is more often found in the countless small choices that shape our lives. It is intentional disciplined practice in the ordinariness of life that makes lovingkindness an integral part of character.

Two beginning points need to be made before we consider twelve more specific and practical dimensions of lovingkindness. First, an act in itself is not sufficient. An apparently kind act done grudgingly or unintentionally (grudgingkindness?) is not offered with a loving frame of mind. Lovingkindness is kind action with loving intention. Just as intention without action falls short, so also kind action without loving intention is incomplete. A smile may be offered for many reasons: friendship, seduction, humor, manipulation, greeting, deception, appreciation, or gloating. Your intention matters. Second, what constitutes kind or loving action depends greatly on context, culture, timing, and individual differences. There are situations where the loving thing to do is to speak and others where it is to be silent. Lovingkindness is not a list of specific prescribed acts but rather intentional choices made with interest in and compassion for another's well-being.

Twelve Choices

Every day you make countless choices, mostly small, that over time become your habits and character. The path of action that you choose at each such fork in the road is not predetermined. To be sure, habits are influenced by many factors such as media and advertising, the models you have seen in your parents and friends, and your genetic makeup, but influence is not destiny. These are choices still. Richard Rohr has observed that "if you don't choose daily and deliberately to practice loving kindness, it is unlikely that a year from now you will be any more loving."

A first step is to become more mindful about daily life, to be conscious that you are, in fact, making these choices among different possible courses of action. It is awareness that you are constantly choosing among forward, neutral, and reverse gears. This is quite different from being on automatic pilot and experiencing life as if you were just reacting naturally to whatever comes your way. It requires attention to and reflection on what you are doing, to the alternatives before you. This is the intentional component of lovingkindness. It is consciousness that you are acting, could act otherwise, and are responsible for the choices you are making. Someone who lacks this capacity is legally insane, but it is quite common to underuse this faculty, living and acting without mindful reflection and awareness of choice. A minimal element is to allow a bit of reflection time before responding "naturally."

For the action component, consider this list of twelve dimensions of choice ranging from examples of humanity (lovingkindness) on the left, through neutrality in the middle, and inhumanity at the far end—the same character continuum described in chapter 2.

HUMANE	NEUTRAL	INHUMANE
Compassionate	Indifferent	Cruel
Empathic	Apathetic	Adversarial
Contented	Discontented	Envious
Generous	Self-Centered	Greedy
Hopeful	Objective	Pessimistic
Affirming	Ignoring	Demeaning
Forgiving	Resentful	Vengeful
Patient	Impatient	Intolerant
Humble	Immodest	Arrogant
Grateful	Unappreciative	Entitled
Helpful	Unhelpful	Obstructive
Yielding	Unyielding	Dominating

Any such list is bound to spark questions and objections. Are these really opposites? Why are some apparent opposites in the neutral column? Aren't there times when being _____ isn't really humane (or inhumane)? Such reflection is a purposeful product of this list. The basic point is that there *are* such dimensions along which we make choices every day and one possible choice is the path of lovingkindness.

These character dimensions are the organizing subjects of chapters 6–17, which reflect on each of these aspects of loving-kindness. I do not mean this list to be exhaustive, including every possible aspect. The list is simply a tool, a starting point for considering ways in which lovingkindness can be practiced in everyday life. With each chapter I offer some possible exercises for realizing an aspect of lovingkindness. "Realizing" here has the double meaning of becoming conscious and of actualizing or putting into practice. Some forms of realizing will fit you better than others. It's just a menu of options to try out and see what helps you move toward your true self of lovingkindness.

But first we consider some common obstacles to realizing lovingkindness.

5

Some Obstacles to Lovingkindness

Just as lovingkindness is a habit of mind and heart, there are competing habits that can obstruct it. This chapter describes a few common hindrances as well as some corresponding remedies.

Inattention

You cannot practice lovingkindness when you're not present. A prerequisite for lovingkindness is paying attention, a mindfulness of the world around you. A perpetual obstacle for me is that I pass through daily life inside my own head focusing on thoughts and feelings, revisiting memories of the past, and rehearsing for the future. I can literally walk or bicycle or drive through a neighborhood while noticing almost nothing that I pass. My wife and I have a standing joke when we're traveling together. She asks me, "Did you notice the . . . ? Oh, never mind." She already knows that the answer is likely to be "no."

The essence of mindfulness is to be fully present in and paying attention to the moment, observing and noticing without judging. For someone like me, that requires practice and discipline. The practice of mindfulness meditation has ancient roots and is being rediscovered in both religious[17] and secular circles.[18]

Regular contemplative practice fosters presence in the moment and a centeredness of being that is an important counterbalance to constant doing. Quakers, whose religious practices are among the most inward-focused and contemplative, also have a venerable history of compassionate action on behalf of others. Compassion fatigue, burnout, and cynicism are potential hazards for those who serve without the grounding of centered mindfulness that makes it possible to sustain lovingkindness.

Beyond the well-documented benefits of mindfulness meditation in physical, mental, and spiritual health there are also meditations focused specifically on fostering and deepening compassion.[19] These have been well described in many other sources and I will not elaborate on this important contemplative aspect of lovingkindness. In this book I am focusing on the practical action side, the living out of lovingkindness.

Fear and Anger

Beyond inattention another hindrance is holding onto negative emotions that can inhibit or distract from lovingkindness. One example is the flight emotions of fear, worry, and anxiety. When preoccupied with pulling away from or avoiding something it is difficult to approach and embrace. There are common barriers of fear and discomfort to overcome before getting to know and be trusted by marginalized people such as those experiencing homelessness, poverty, addiction, or incarceration. Fear and love tend to drive each other away.

Then there are the hot emotions of resentment, bitterness, anger, and hatred that can also impede lovingkindness. Unlike the moving-away of fear and its kin, these are moving-against emotions and for present purposes they have two interesting attributes. First, they are often reactions to avoidant emotions of pain, fear, or both. When startled we may snap back. If suddenly experiencing pain two animals in a cage will often attack each other. With people it may not be physical pain (although it can be) that triggers anger but the emotional pain of a criticism, rejection, or loss.

Feeling hurt turns into a desire to hurt back. Someone in traffic "cuts us off" or honks a horn and we may fume. We don't like being hurt or startled, and either emotion can quickly turn into anger and later resentment. When feeling angry it can be useful to consider what could be the underlying emotion. Second, the hot emotions require fairly constant fueling. Without access to more fuel or oxygen a fire will soon go out. In order to remain angry or resentful one must mentally refresh perceived offenses or hurts. Let go of this refueling process and the fire dies down. Over time, however, the refueling process can become unconscious and habitual. Anger-prone and aggressive people, for example, tend to systematically misperceive anger and enmity in other people's facial expressions.[20]

The Prison of Privilege

Privilege is a third potential obstacle to lovingkindness. A rather consistent theme in spiritual teachings is that wealth and power, the trappings of worldly success, are hazardous to your spiritual health. Why is that?

In the dynamics of oppression both parties are in need of liberation. Inequality and oppression are bad for all concerned. Though always worse for the oppressed, there is a complementary captivity for those with the upper hand who are themselves on a slavish road to ruin that might be called the prison of privilege. A vexing aspect of this prison is that we may not even recognize its walls as limiting.

The book *The Spirit Level* meticulously documented how both rich and poor fare worse when they live in a more unequal society, one in which there is a large income gap between rich and poor. Currently in the United States the top 20 percent earn on average at least nine times as much as the bottom 20 percent—the highest level of income inequality since 1929 and one of the most disparate in the world among developed nations. When my father worked for the Reading Railroad in the 1950s, his salary was about one-tenth of that for an executive. Now in some corporations a

CEO earns five hundred to a thousand times more than the average salary of employees, a ratio that rivals medieval feudalism. Such injustice is clearly much harder on the poor, but the rich also pay a price for inequality in society. On average as a people we are (whether rich or poor) less healthy, more obese, more depressed and anxious, take more psychiatric medications, have more teen pregnancies and infant mortality, more violence and homicide, more prisons, more alcohol/drug problems, and die younger in direct proportion to the size of the gap between rich and poor.[21] These problems are not driven by the average level of income in a state or industrialized country but by the degree of income inequality. People at the same income level in more equal societies fare far better on all these measures. Living in an unjust society is bad for all of us.

Poverty is neither necessary nor inevitable.[22] It is not essential to have people living in want so that others can be prosperous. It is not necessary for some people to go hungry or be homeless. It is only gross inequality that fosters deprivation: when some become far wealthier relative to the population, others become far poorer. It is self-promotion at the expense of and to the neglect of others that is oppression.

I suggest that there are four walls to the prison of privilege, as well as an antidote for each of them. First, there is the wall of *greed*, the sense of urgency to accumulate more resources for oneself. Greed values individual gain over the common good and honors people for what they have—and drive, and wear, and live in—rather than for what they do for their community. From this perspective the ultimate good is to get and keep for oneself as much as possible and build bigger barns to hold it all. A good antidote for greed is *generosity*. Giving away generously is a preventive vaccine for greed (see chapter 9).

Second, there is the wall of *anxiety*. Sometimes we are driven not by outright greed *per se* but by its avoidant cousin, the fear that we will not have enough and will be on our own with no one to help us. This anxiety is particularly strong among those who have already lived through hard times. It can be a fairly constant nagging worry that is exacerbated as economic inequality increases. Here there is the antidote of *simplicity*. The more stuff we accumulate, the more time and worry and resources we must devote to storing, protecting, and maintaining it. Possessions can come to possess us. Beyond the basic needs and a little more, additional money and stuff do not make people any happier as individuals or as a society. Shopping brings no more enduring happiness than snorting a line of cocaine or playing a video game. The less we have, the less we have to worry about. Simplicity alleviates anxiety.

A third wall of the prison of privilege is *entitlement*. First we become accustomed to privilege, then we no longer see or enjoy it as privilege and start believing that we are entitled to or even need it. "I deserve what I have and more! I have it coming to me. It's mine—it belongs to me." A spiritual remedy here is *gratitude*, to be actively thankful for that which we do have (see chapter 15). When experiencing and expressing appreciation for the gifts that we do have we're less likely to crave more. It is also useful to have a periodic dose of humility. A friend of mine in Alcoholics Anonymous exclaims, "Thank God we don't get what we deserve!"

Lastly, there is the prison wall of *envy*, of wanting what others have. This, too, is exacerbated by economic disparity. Greater social inequity in possessions and lifestyle tends to foster jealousy, which has an interesting double meaning. Jealousy means both resentment of others' advantage and vigilance in protecting one's own advantage. Once again, both captives and captors are enslaved. An antidote to the poison of envy is the spirituality of *enough*, to be content with and grateful for what we have, which is usually far more than sufficient (see chapter 8).

Greed, anxiety, entitlement, and envy: these are walls of the prison of privilege. Generosity, simplicity, gratitude, and contentment: these are keys to the prison door.

May you place your trust in that which does not crumble. May you have a peace that no amount of prosperity, comfort, security, or success can ever take away.

6

Compassion

Compassionate   Indifferent   Cruel

Compassion—the first of the twelve aspects listed in chapter 4—is a central characteristic of lovingkindness. It is not a feeling like sympathy so much as an intention: to alleviate suffering and contribute to the well-being of others. As an intention it is reflected in action. The best of intentions are of little use to anyone else unless and until they are enacted. There is an inner experience and then corresponding behavior by which it is realized—made real.

The inner intention of compassion as a basic starting point is one component of the Hippocratic oath: "First, do no harm." Within Buddhism, the same intention is just the first of four steps:

- to prevent any evil from starting,

- to remove any evil as soon as it starts,

- to induce the doing of good deeds, and

- to encourage the growth and continuance of good deeds already begun.

Nonviolence is an unambiguous central theme in the teachings of both Jesus and the Buddha, as it was in the work of Mohandas Gandhi and Martin Luther King Jr. Loving even your enemies implies first of all not harming them. This intention is realized in refraining from cruel acts that could hurt, wound, or dehumanize others.

More common than outright cruelty are smaller acts of unkindness, sometimes called *microaggression*. Just abstaining from unkind action is itself a challenging aspiration. One step in the right direction is to have a positive and increasing ratio of kind to unkind acts. When counseling couples in distressed relationships I often started by having them list and mind their "Ps and Ds"— pleases and displeases—as defined by each other. What is it that pleases and displeases your partner? Each person begins counting the Ps and Ds that they give and receive, seeking to offer more Ps and fewer Ds. At the beginning of counseling, distressed couples are usually exchanging far more Ds than Ps.

In between compassionate (forward gear) and cruel (reverse) is neutrality, time that is spent with neither intention. Neutral gear occupies a large proportion of time and life for most people. This includes important self-care time for sleeping, resting, taking care of basic personal needs, socializing, leisure, play, and exercise. It is certainly possible to spend too little time in such self-care. There may also be some large spans of discretionary neutral time (such as watching TV, playing games, or surfing electronic media) that could be spent instead in compassionate care for others including friends, family and loved ones, the community, and those in need.

It's an honest inventory to ask what proportion of your time you have been spending in these three gears over the past few months: forward (compassionate action), neutral, and reverse (unkind, cruel, or harmful action). Think of it as a pie chart. How does it look?

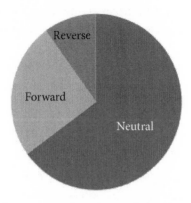

Keep this pie chart in mind in this and the chapters that follow. Each chapter addresses one of the twelve character dimensions listed in chapter 4. For each dimension you can consider the balance in your own life currently among time spent in each of the three gears. In this chapter the balance is among being compassionate (forward), indifferent (neutral), and unkind or cruel (reverse).

A compassionate act is one that is intended to contribute to the well-being of another, sometimes at cost to yourself. It communicates caring and support for the person's welfare and happiness. The easiest examples are acts on behalf of those who are in need, such as sending a compassionate card or letter, feeding the hungry, or visiting those who are sick or incarcerated. These are not heroic deeds requiring great personal sacrifice. They are simple acts on behalf of another.

So where do you start if you wish to move forward a bit in the practice of lovingkindness? How can you devote more time to compassionate action and less to indifference or unkindness? In Boy Scouting, younger (Cub) Scouts have as their slogan, "Do a good deed daily." There is a simple beginning. Start with a goal of adding at least one intentional kindness each day. On most days that is fairly easy, and it's a place to start. Don't feel restricted, of course. You need not stop at one; that's just a minimum, and don't worry too much about what counts. Just begin moving in the right direction. As Scouts grow older their "law" expands to, "Be kind to others at all times"—a challenging goal toward which to grow. One way to get a sense of your progress is to count your own Ps and Ds toward other people in the course of a day. How's your balance?

Taking Care of Yourself

Just for clarity, it is not a wise goal to eliminate as much neutral time as possible, to get less sleep and have no rest, leisure, or fun time so that it can all be spent doing for others. If you make yourself ill, depressed, or otherwise disabled you diminish your ability to be helpful at all. The airline warning is wise: put your own oxygen mask on first and then assist others. Now, many people do have plenty of room to move before this becomes a concern, but there also are those already devoting most of their time to taking care of other people and not themselves. The advice to "love your neighbor as yourself" implies compassion for yourself as well as others. I am writing this book for people who may want to move in the direction of spending more time on the path of lovingkindness. If you're already spread thin and stressed by caring for others, the most loving change you can make might be to take better care of yourself.

Is Lovingkindness a Sickness?

In the 1990s there grew out of the addiction field the concept of "codependence." Initially the belief was that family members of people experiencing addiction have a progressive illness themselves with complementary personality patterns that need to maintain the person's illness. The lists of "symptoms" of codependence became so broad that many people could identify with it, and indeed some writings averred that a vast majority of adults suffer from the illness of codependence. Compassionate action itself could be suspect and disparaged as pathological. An effort to have codependence classified as a diagnosable and treatable disorder was rejected by the American Psychiatric Association for lack of any scientific evidence that such an illness exists.

The kernel of truth here is that people and families sometimes can inadvertently, and with the best of intentions, fall into protective patterns that make it easier for their loved one to continue in self-destructive behavior. Some find the concept of codependence helpful in raising awareness of one's own participation in destructive patterns. The intention of such "enabling" behavior is compassionate but the actual effect is harmful. This pattern has been understood since the 1950s as a normal adjustment of families responding to the crisis of addiction, and it is not indicative of any larger personality disorder.[23] Compassion is not a sickness, although unintended consequences can occur. The key is to examine the actual (not just intended) effects of your actions on others, and this is wise in all our affairs.

Realizing

Daily Life

Suppose you decided to add one simple act of lovingkindness each day. What things could you actually do? It might be as simple as sending a note or making a telephone call. Make a list of possibilities, and don't censor as you go. The idea is to make a long list of *possible* acts of lovingkindness that you could fit into your days.

In your daily life, who are some people who might benefit from simple loving acts from you? Again, make a list including not only those you already love but others you may not know or with whom you may have felt conflict or resentment.

Bigger Picture

Thinking about your life over the past few months or perhaps the past year, how would you draw your own pie chart of time spent in forward (compassionate), neutral (indifferent), and reverse (hurtful) gears? This can be an interesting exercise at the end of each year. If you were to draw another pie chart for how you would like (realistically) to be spending your gear time, how would it look?

Self-Care

Who offers lovingkindness to you? Are there loving people with whom you could spend more time? In what ways may you need to be more compassionate with yourself? Write yourself a reminder note.

7

Empathy

Empathic   Apathetic   Adversarial

As with compassion, empathy is sometimes thought of as just an inner feeling like sympathy. The vital human capacity for empathy is far larger than that and it has at least two important elements. One element of empathy is internal and motivational—a *desire* to understand someone else's perspective and experience. People vary widely in this aspect of empathy. Did you have a "cookie person" when you were growing up—someone who always seemed glad to see you, who was interested in listening to you and often offered little acts of kindness like warm cookies?

A second component of empathy is a skill, the *ability* to accurately understand other people and perceive the world through their eyes. You may be able to imagine what someone might be feeling or thinking at a particular moment (as in watching a movie), but the skill of empathy goes beyond imagination by seeking to get it right, to correctly understand at least part of what a person is actually experiencing. As human beings we have a hardwired capacity for this: to be able to "read" people, to guess what they may be thinking or feeling. Some folks are much better at this than others, and it is possible to strengthen this skill, to learn how to do it better. I will come back to that later in this chapter.

Empathic concern and empathic skill don't necessarily go together. It is possible to be high on either one and low on the other. A person might be very good at accurately understanding other people but not very interested in doing so. Even enemies and competitors, though, are often interested in accurately reading their adversaries' thoughts and feelings, if only for self-serving reasons. You may also know people who are curious about and interested in people but are not very good at understanding someone else's perspective.

The neutral zone on the dimension of empathic concern is apathy: not being interested in or caring about the experience of others. At the far end from empathic concern is antipathy: an antagonistic or adversarial rejection of the experience of others. In a state of antipathy one might listen to another person just long enough to decide what is wrong with their perspective and how to disagree. As with the other character dimensions you have a choice about how much time and effort to spend in the forward (empathic), neutral (apathetic), and reverse (adversarial) gears.

What about empathic ability, the skill of accurate understanding? For forty years I have studied and taught accurate empathy as a foundational communication skill in the training of psychologists and other helpers. Most people, I found, were able to start learning and practicing this skill at a beginning level over the course of a few months. There were a few individuals whom I was unable to teach, and the shortcoming may well have been mine, but even after a significant amount of coaching they didn't seem able to perceive the world from any perspective other than their own. They had empathic concern but not the ability.

A fundamental insight underlying empathic skill is that there are at least three steps where any communication can go wrong, as illustrated in the chart below. Whenever people speak there is a meaning behind what they say, what they are thinking and feeling at the moment (Circle 1). Then they put their meaning into words (Circle 2), and as you know, people don't always say exactly what they mean. Next you have to hear the words correctly (Circle 3). You can mishear for many reasons: for example, if you're not paying close attention, are listening in a second language, have some hearing loss or a bad phone connection. Then you need to run whatever words you hear through your own mental dictionary and history of experience. What does the person mean? (Circle 4)

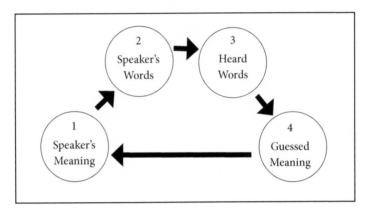

In other words, with any one communication there are at least three places where it can go wrong. Yet most people respond as if Circle 4 were the same as Circle 1, believing that what they think the words they thought they heard could mean is what the speaker actually meant.

Circle 1: Boss's meaning: "I want that letter sent right away."
Circle 2: Boss's words (through an office door ajar): "Would you send that letter?"
Circle 3: What the assistant heard: "Did you send that letter?"
Circle 4: Assistant's reply: "No."

Already things are off to a bad start, with a breakdown at Circle 3. The boss could have been clearer at Circle 2: "I'd like you to send that letter right away please." But there is another way for the listener to keep communication on the right track, represented by the long arrow from Circle 4 to Circle 1, and that is to make a guess about what the speaker meant. It could be asked as a question: "Do you mean the letter to Boston?" But asking people what they mean all the time gets old very quickly. A better approach is to say what you think the person means, to actually make your guess as a statement rather than a question.

Boss: Would you send that letter?
Assistant: You want the letter to Boston to go out today.
Boss: Oh, not the Boston letter. The one I gave you this morning.
Assistant: Oh, the letter to Dr. Jenkins.
Boss: Yes. Please get it in the mail today.
Assistant: OK, I will.

This is a fairly simple misunderstanding that is easily corrected. The usefulness of this skill of empathic understanding is even greater in personal communications, like this one between friends. The listener (L) is working hard to understand what the friend (F) means.

F. I'm just about at the end of my rope.
L: It's been a pretty rough day. (A guess, though asking, "What's wrong?" could be OK.)
F: Well yes, but it's more than just today. I'm really worried about Alicia.
L: Your daughter! It's been rough with her for quite a while.
F: The school called again and said she didn't show up this morning.
L: Oh dear! You don't know where she went if she wasn't there.
F: Not yet. I'm going to ask her but that probably won't go well.
L: Depending how you ask her, I suppose.
F: Well, right, but if I try to tiptoe around something like this I don't get anything.
L: And you want to know where she really was. You're concerned.
F: This just keeps happening. I go along thinking things are going well, and then this.
L: You get your hopes up . . .
F: And then she disappoints me again. I don't know what to do anymore.
L: How can I be your friend right now? What can I do?
F: You're doing it right now.

Up until the last question (empathic concern) the listener has been making guesses in the form of statements, and pretty good ones at that, about what the friend's words mean and the feelings and experiences beneath the words.

Notice also that there are quite a few things that the listener is not doing, things that psychologist Thomas Gordon called roadblocks to good listening,[24] like:

- Giving advice or making suggestions (Have you tried . . .)
- Warning or telling what to do (You'd better . . .)
- Asking a lot of questions (How old is she? Who are her friends?)
- Reassuring (I'm sure this will turn out all right.)
- Explaining (She's just going through a phase.)
- Distracting, changing the subject (Did you see the news this morning?)

These are called roadblocks because they make it harder for the person to continue talking from the heart. They interrupt, redirect, or say, "I've heard enough. Now listen to me." Instead of doing any of these roadblocks the listener keeps seeking to understand more clearly while also expressing empathic concern.

This looks simple but it is not an easy skill. People who are good at it make it look easy, but it takes practice to stop asking so many questions, resist the tempting roadblocks (even if intended to be helpful), and keep seeking to understand the other's experience, making sure that Circle 4 is what the person means. It is deep, patient, high-quality listening like this that develops skillfulness in accurate empathy.

Beyond this practical skill, the inner experience of accurate empathy involves a curiosity about people, a desire to learn and understand. If you are not really interested in people you are unlikely to take the time and effort required to enter into their own experience. It is this open curiosity combined with empathic concern that make a true friend, companion, counselor, or soul mate.

To do this with strangers, those with whom you have no history or relationship, is more rare still and a true gift. Henri Nouwen wrote that "anyone who willingly enters into the pain of a stranger is truly a remarkable person."[25] At the intersection of accurate understanding and empathic concern, there is lovingkindness.

Realizing

Listening to Yourself Listening

Most people believe that they are good listeners and perhaps you do, too. When you are trying to be a good listener, what are you actually doing? Is your full attention focused on understanding the other person's experience? To what extent are you putting up roadblocks as listed in this chapter? Imagine that a friend said this to you: "I just feel so discouraged. I keep trying to make this relationship work, but every time I get my hopes up he starts criticizing me again." Quick: What is the first thing that comes to your mind to say?

For most people, the first thing that comes to mind is a roadblock like asking a question, reassuring, or advising. What could you say instead that would be an empathic guess about what your friend means or feels?

Gear Time

Thinking about your life over the past few months, how might you draw your own pie chart of time you have spent in forward (empathic), neutral (apathetic or superficial), and reverse (adversarial) gears during your conversations?

Perhaps it differs depending on the person with whom you're talking. Think about a particular person in your life with whom you often converse. What does your pie chart look like with that person? How about with different kinds of people with whom you interact?

Empathic Listening

What a loving gift it is just to listen to someone with no other purpose than to understand who they are and what they mean! To whom do you listen in this way? Who listens to you like this?

Try it out. The next time you are having a conversation with someone, think of your sole purpose as being to understand what the person thinks, feels, and means. There is no need for you to agree or disagree, advise or suggest, be clever or console. Just focus on understanding accurately. Instead of asking questions, try mirroring—offering short summary statements of what you think the person may mean or be experiencing. Don't make big interpretive leaps (which can be a roadblock), and also don't just repeat like a parrot. Your goal is to make small guesses and understand. In essence, you are saying what might be the *next* sentence in the paragraph, and there's no penalty for guessing incorrectly. People just pick up where you left off and tell you more about what they *do* mean!

Intentionally practice this skill of listening deeply with a friend, with no agenda except to understand what he or she means and is experiencing. It can deepen friendship.

In Conflict

Focused listening to gain accurate understanding can be especially challenging when you disagree or are in a conflict situation. It can also be particularly important at these times. In such situations, first make sure that you understand and can state the other person's perspective. "Let me see if I understand what you mean . . . " No sarcasm or attitude! Just take as long as needed to make sure that you understand. Then express your own perspective and ask the other person to summarize what you have said.

8

Contentment

Contented   Discontented   Envious

Lovingkindness is joyful, and the delight is not in what has been or what may be but in contented acceptance of what is. One marker on the path of lovingkindness is the joyful experience of *enough*, to celebrate and be content with whatever is. An oft-quoted Buddhist proverb is that "enough is a feast." The Apostle Paul wrote, "I have learned to be content whatever the circumstances. I know what it is to be in need, and I know what it is to have plenty. I have learned the secret of being content in any and every situation."[26]

This is not at all the same as complacency or lack of aspirations. Rather, it is the peace of letting today be sufficient for today. Buddhism teaches mindfulness, to pay attention to and appreciate whatever is in the present moment. Indeed, we have no other moment. Yesterday is gone and when tomorrow arrives it will be today. The cost of living in the past or the future is to miss enjoying and appreciating what is here now. This is one thing that Dickens's Ebenezer Scrooge learned from his ghosts.

The central or neutral position on this dimension is discontentment with the current situation no matter what it is. This is rather like cats who, regardless of their position relative to a closed door, are always on the wrong side of it.

Discontent opens the door to the opposite of an "enough" mind, which is envy and jealousy, to resent or want what others have. How striking that "do not covet" stands among the Ten Commandments alongside prohibitions against murder, theft, perjury, and adultery! Perhaps it is because covetousness is so often a motivation for the rest.

There is much in the modern and postmodern world that cultivates envy. Economic disparity fosters it. It is the very essence of advertising to persuade us that our present circumstances are inadequate, that we should want and have what we do not truly need. Ads and commercials promise happiness but what they offer is typically transient at best if not an outright lie. Alcohol ads, for example, tend to imply that drinking a particular product is associated with being rich, attractive, popular, successful, sexy, fit, healthy, and happy—an empty promise and often the opposite of the truth.

The hunger for more is an insatiable beast and shopping does not placate it for long. The Buddha emphasized that this hunger is a primary source of suffering for ourselves and others. In our consumer culture, Americans buy and eat and work and drink far more than needed, dying from obesity in a world where millions perish from starvation. So long as "more" is the goal there can never be enough. The belief that "if I can just get more [*fill in the blank*], then I'll be satisfied" is an illusion and becomes an endless treadmill. Having acquired more of whatever it is, one is still unsatisfied and concludes that even more must be necessary. Happiness is not about more. It is about enough, and that opens the door, the time and space for lovingkindness.

Simplicity—to "keep it simple"—is a discipline of the "enough" mind that questions whether more is truly any better, be it in regard to speech, food, progress, comfort, fame, friends, possessions, work, privileges, appearance, or achievements.[27] Abraham Lincoln's profound Gettysburg Address was just two minutes long and quickly overshadowed the featured two-hour oration that preceded it. Beyond having a minimum level of resources needed for sustenance, the amount of additional money or goods that people possess is simply unrelated to their degree of life satisfaction and happiness. Having more "stuff" just requires more space in which to store it and often more effort and resources to maintain, move, and protect it.[28]

Realizing

Dayenu

The *Dayenu* is a thousand-year-old song that is part of the Jewish celebration of *Pesach* or Passover. Reciting a sequence of blessings, the essence of each line is that "it would already have been enough if God had only . . . " In this way, it is an ancient form of the common advice to count your blessings.

Choose some aspect of your life in which you may experience a need for *more*. For me, at various times in my own life, it has been money, work, publications, approval, and recognition. (If you are familiar with the Enneagram,[29] I am a 3.) Make a list of the ways in which you have already been blessed in this area, perhaps in chronological order. It may work well to write each one on a small card or piece of paper so that you can then easily arrange them in order from lesser blessings to greater ones. Then following the rhythm of the *Dayenu*, recite or meditate, pray or chant your way through the list: It would already have been enough if I (or God, or Life) had only [*fill in one blessing*]. The traditional *Dayenu* proceeds through the increasing blessings in sequential pairs: "It would already have been enough if God had only given us [*one blessing*] and not [*the next blessing*]." Save your list and experiment with different ways of meditating through it.

Fasting

For thousands of years world religions have advocated fasting—voluntarily refraining from particular comforts or behavior for a period of time. The term is most often associated with abstaining from food, but the practice can be applied to any desired and habitual behavior: work (as in observing a Sabbath), sex, sweets, alcohol, TV, or social media. The purpose is not to inflict suffering; quite the opposite. It is interesting, though, that this long-standing and common spiritual practice has fallen into such disuse in our culture of immediate gratification.

Choose something that you do regularly, habitually, even for good reasons (like eating or working), something that takes up your time. When I have fasted from food I have been amazed at the amount of time in one day normally spent in buying, choosing, preparing, and eating food and cleaning up afterward. One thing often learned is that you don't *have* to do the thing from which you are fasting. You can let it go and the sky doesn't fall. It also strengthens your self-control "muscles" that can atrophy when you give in automatically to desires.[30]

Choose a period of time to fast from your chosen habit. A weekend or holiday can be a total fast from work. A food fast can be for one meal, one day, or several days. In world religions there are fast days (like the Jewish *Yom Kippur*), months (like the Muslim *Ramadan*), or even longer periods (like the Christian *Lent*). What length of time do you choose to interrupt your usually desired practice? Take reasonable care, of course, not to harm yourself or someone else in the process; for example, don't get dehydrated or hypoglycemic.

Finally, don't rebound at the end of your fast. It can be tempting to make up for lost time, to compensate by gorging on what you've missed. In breaking a food fast (literally breakfast) the usual advice is to eat a very modest meal. Ease back into your regular pattern, or perhaps you will decide to change it. I recently found myself too engrossed in computer solitaire and had begun playing most every day sometimes for an hour or more. I chose this as my fast for Lent—forty-six days during which I noticed how often I *would* have played. After the fast I gave myself permission to play again, but before long I was once more mindlessly wasting large chunks of time, so I uninstalled the solitaire software from my laptop. I still notice habitual urges when I probably would have played "just one" had it been there, but here I am writing this book instead.

Refraining

Akin to fasting is a shorter practice of intentionally refraining from a habitual desired behavior in a situation where it would almost certainly occur otherwise. Psychologists call this exposure with response prevention. For example, go into a fast food restaurant you enjoy but don't order anything. Sit down, smell the food, watch other people eating but don't eat, then walk out after twenty minutes or so. Or go into a store or shopping center where you almost always buy something, spend time looking at products on offer, then go home without buying anything. Again, don't put yourself at risk. If it helps, take along a friend who understands what you are doing and just have a conversation. The point is to practice breaking the automatic link between desire and action.

9

Generosity

Generous   Self-Centered   Greedy

Generosity is a willingness or joy to share what you have with others, to give more than is necessary or expected. To practice generosity is a choice precisely because it is not compulsory. Doing only what is expected or required is no virtue. (Remember from chapter 3: "If you love only those who love you, what *kharis*, what credit is that to you?")

Generosity follows naturally from a deep and secure sense of *enough* (chapter 8) as well as a perspective of common wealth and our interconnectedness with each other. Some of the most generous people I know have been homeless; when they have something they share it, in part because that's how you survive. ("You need this more than I do.") They rarely carry more than they need. I remember offering an extra shirt to a friend who had finally managed to get into an apartment after twenty years of surviving on the street. "What do I need a second shirt for?" he asked me, not with irritation but with curiosity. He genuinely did not understand a need to have more than one shirt at a time.

In traveling I have found the same, that some of the most generous people I meet are those with few personal resources. During the Soviet era I was walking with five friends down a street in Krasnodar, Russia. An old woman was out sweeping her sidewalk with a broom made from bound twigs and when she heard our English her eyes grew wide and she grasped our arms. Our translator said that she wanted us to come to dinner the next night, and she was not about to take "no" for an answer. When we returned she crowded the six of us at a low table in her tiny living room while curious neighbors packed around us. It became apparent that she had been up much of the night preparing mounds of *blini,* delicious pancakes that she served us with fresh applesauce and cabbage. A retired music teacher, she then regaled us for an hour with Russian torch songs accompanying herself on a concertina. The food must have cost her dearly on a meager budget, and nobody else ate until we had departed into the night with a memory to last a lifetime.

A midpoint on this character dimension is self-centeredness, "looking out for number one," amassing more than one's actual need. There are large differences in how much people believe they need. Since the 1980s the average footprint of American homes has more than doubled, necessitating growing indebtedness. Selfishness can be fueled by competitiveness, by a sense of scarcity (that there is not enough to go around), or by individualism (that we are all on our own and must look out for ourselves). An anxious hunger to keep acquiring more is part of the prison of privilege (chapter 5).

At the far point from generosity is greed, acquiring excess by depriving others. One example is theft, stealing for personal gain. Greed combines selfishness with a lack of concern for others. It can be a personal practice but greed can also be built into social systems that, like feudalism, amass gains for a few at the expense of many. World cultures vary in their sense of mutual responsibility and providing for each other's welfare. More collectivist nations prize welfare of the community or society over individual goals, the common good over private good.

Generosity is not limited to money and material resources. We also give others the treasure of our time, skills, and expertise. For example, one can be generous or stingy with recognition, affection, manual skills, affirmation, mentoring, and acts of kindness. "I don't have time" can be a reality and also a choice. In truth, we all have the same amount of time in a day or year and decide how to spend it. People in subsistence cultures have fewer choices, necessarily devoting most of their time to survival. More affluent nations offer ample leisure, and "screen time" (TV, computers, phones, movies, and such) can occupy large swaths of life time. Addiction (be it to drugs, exercise, the internet, work, pornography, sex, or gambling) involves giving ever more of one's time and resources to something that is unworthy of central devotion—a clear modern example of idolatry.

Taking an honest look at yourself, a "searching and fearless moral inventory," is not an easy task. It is far more comfortable not to think too much about aspects of yourself that in your heart you know you need or ought to change. These chapters invite you to consider where you actually spend your time and energy on each of the twelve character dimensions introduced in chapter 4. Wherever you are at present on these dimensions is not where you must remain. Although it does happen in real life (as described in chapter 1), few of us have sudden and dramatic transformations of the Ebenezer Scrooge variety and it's wise not to wait for one. Mark Twain observed that "habit is habit and not to be flung out of the window by any[one], but coaxed downstairs a step at a time." Generosity is practiced one small action at a time, as if moving into a future that is coming when all shall be well.

Realizing

Slicing the Pie

How do you spend your life? Draw a pie chart for what occupies significant portions of your waking hours. How did you actually spend your time yesterday? The categories are yours to choose, but to what are you currently giving your time? Are there pieces of the pie that you believe ought to be smaller or larger? Similarly, you can draw a pie chart for how you spend money. Look at financial records—what are the largest items on your credit card and bank statements? This reflects your values. Organizational and governmental budgets are also moral documents, very concretely valuing certain expenditures over others. What pieces of the pie might you choose to make smaller or larger in your own (or organizational) time and finances?

Practicing Generosity

What do you have that you might give away to someone who needs or would appreciate it? Suppose you decided to practice greater generosity with your time, care, money, food, skills, or possessions. One woman decided to try fasting from criticizing others and instead to look for ways to offer affirmation (see chapter 11). It could even be practicing more generosity with yourself by taking needed time for rest and regeneration—to observe a true Sabbath.[31]

A Cheerful Giver

Generosity should be a joyful rather than begrudging act. What do you *enjoy* giving to others? What is it that when you give it away, you feel happier, stronger, or more like the person you want to be? For those on the receiving end, it is a much better experience to receive from someone who truly enjoys being generous than from one who practices it reluctantly or resentfully.

Sometimes you may need to give yourself the opportunity, because you can't enjoy what you haven't tried. What kind of generosity might you enjoy practicing, and with whom?

10

Hope

Hopeful   Objective   Pessimistic

In appreciation for allowing them to do psychological testing in three alcoholism treatment programs, researchers offered the staff some feedback regarding their patients by identifying those who had particularly high alcohol recovery potential (HARP) according to their test results. Their predictions turned out to be remarkably accurate. At discharge the staff rated HARPs as having been more motivated and cooperative, more punctual in attending appointments, neater in appearance, showing better self-control, and working harder for their sobriety. Over the year following discharge the HARPs were indeed more likely to be employed, to remain abstinent, to have fewer slips and longer spans of recovery. Pretty accurate tests? No, in fact the patients identified as HARPs had been chosen at random. They were no different from other patients on prior treatment history or severity of problems. The only difference was that the staff working with them had been told that these people were going to recover particularly well.[32]

Hope is a powerful healer. Why is it that new medications have to be tested against placebo, so that neither provider nor

44

patient knows whether the capsule contains the actual medicine or inert ingredients? It is because simply receiving a treatment with hope of benefit can promote substantial healing. Our expectations have a way of coming true, not always but often.[33] As Henry Ford observed, "Whether you think you can, or you think you can't— you're right."

This chapter is here in a book on lovingkindness because as illustrated in the true story that opens this chapter, hope affects not only yourself but those whose lives you touch. To be hopeful is to look for the best, not because of and often in spite of the current evidence. It has been said that there is no such thing as false hope and in an important sense it is true, because hope itself can inspire change even though it may seem ridiculous. It is the transformative madness of Don Quixote in *Man of La Mancha* who stubbornly perceives the prostitute Aldonza to be the noble Lady Dulcinea. It can be a gift, albeit not always welcomed, to see in others possibilities that they do not see in themselves. When I ask people to remember and tell about their favorite teacher this is one characteristic they often remember and appreciate: She (or he) saw and brought out in me something I did not know I had. Several of my professors did this for me. One was my music professor at Lycoming College. I was very nervous when I went to audition as a freshman for the college choir. He struck a key on his grand piano and said, "Sing this note on 'Ah.'" I did my best as he proceeded up the scale in half steps until I reached my upper limit and said, "That's all I can do." "Oh my, no," he replied. "There is much more there. I *like* what I hear! Did you know that you are a first tenor?" In the years that followed, Professor McIver gave me a gift that I would continue to develop and enjoy for the rest of my life.

The forward gear, then, is hopefulness, to anticipate and look expectantly for the best in others, in life, and in the future. One pundit quipped that the opposite of paranoia is *narapoia*: the belief that people are secretly plotting to do you good.

The midpoint or neutral gear on this dimension is sometimes called being objective: to perceive and rely on the present evidence, the current state of affairs. It is the well-intentioned family and friends trying to talk Don Quixote out of his madness. This perspective is also sometimes called "realism," although the term somewhat arrogantly assumes that the perceived present is the only possible reality. Whereas we normally tend to give ourselves the benefit of the doubt, people who are clinically depressed actually tend to have a more realistic appraisal of their own abilities and shortcomings. I once passed through several months of dark depression and to me one of the strongest and strangest indications that something was amiss was that my usual reflexive optimism was gone.

From the viewpoint of objectivity, hope may appear naïve, but again it's a matter of chosen perspective. In a 1963 speech President John F. Kennedy famously paraphrased lines from George Bernard Shaw: "There are those who look at things the way they are, and ask why? I dream of things that never were, and ask why not?" Hopefulness has a way of moving things forward beyond the objective present.

The opposite end of this spectrum is pessimism or cynicism, anticipating the worst. Any of the three positions on this character dimension might be construed as a service to others. When embroiled in administration I had a colleague whose perspective I valued precisely because he was always vigilant for and rather expected the direst possible outcomes from people and situations. He was the canary in the mine, a good complement to my own habitual optimism. I learned not to succumb to his gloomy outlook but I always paid attention to it.

Where you reside on this dimension of hope is a matter of choice. It is not predestined by nature or nurture, by your genes or past experience. It is a chosen spot, a "choice location" if you will. Given a choice to anticipate either the best or the worst in other people I lean toward the former. I do so fully aware that I may be inaccurate. I would be a terrible weather forecaster, but accurate prediction is not the heart of hope. Unlike with weather it *matters* what you choose to believe and predict about people. A virtue in pessimism, it is said, is that you will never be disappointed, and indeed it's true. Both optimism and pessimism tend to become self-fulfilling prophecies.

Realizing

Favorite Teacher

Who was your own favorite teacher, someone in whose class you were motivated or inspired to learn?[34] She or he could be from anywhere along the line in school or even outside the bounds of formal classrooms. If you can't narrow it down to one person, then you're fortunate indeed. Think of several. What was it about them that brought out the best in you? What did they actually do that made them memorable and special for you? Write it down.

And for whom have you been or might you be a person like this as a teacher, coach, encourager, or mentor? How have you been or might you be more like your favorite teacher was for you?

Whispering Hope

Hope is more likely to whisper than to shout, to be a still, small voice that change is possible. What is a situation in your own life about which you now have a choice to be hopeful, objective, or pessimistic? If you did choose to be hopeful, what words, phrases, or sentences of encouragement could you whisper to yourself? Jot them down. Carry them with you.

The Lending Bank of Hope

Whom do you know who may need to borrow some hope from you? When someone seems to lack hope of their own you may be able to lend them some of yours. This is not best done by disagreeing with them ("No, you're wrong. You *can* do this.") or cheerleading, but by offering your own perspective of hope. Think of a particular person who might need to borrow some hope from you.

How might you transfer some of that hope without disagreeing or cheerleading? Write a paragraph of what you might say to this person. You don't have to actually send this message (though it's a possibility), but it's good practice to produce the words.

11

Affirmation

Affirming   Ignoring   Demeaning

Whereas hope foresees positive possibilities, the loving habit of affirmation notices and acknowledges what is already good in the present. It is a disposition to look for and hold onto what is good. The attitude of affirmation is to catch people doing something right, to notice and affirm the positive. But before exploring the forward gear of affirmation, consider the reverse.

The opposite disposition is to be vigilant for and criticize the negative, be it with a person, a situation, or the world more generally. There is something so alluring about negativity, as though it deserved special attention. When I received evaluations of university classes that I had taught I used to quickly leaf through the many positive ones, not really taking time to absorb the personal notes of genuine appreciation. I was scanning for those few from dissatisfied or disgruntled students. These I would carefully study for where I had gone wrong in my teaching, taking in the piercing comments and pondering what I should be doing differently. An ironic aspect of this bias is that changing in response to exceptional negativity may undo what the majority valued and appreciated!

And what glee there can be in catching someone doing something wrong or in seeing the downfall of a prominent or virtuous person! The German word for this guilty pleasure is *Schadenfreude*—to enjoy someone else's shame or misfortune. It is the pandering stuff of gossip, pundits, tabloids, and news media. What is it about negativity that can be so enthralling? Perhaps it is the allure of seeing ourselves as more virtuous or fortunate by comparison.

There are people who just seem to go through life looking for reasons to be angry, to decry and disparage. It is misfortune indeed to have such a drill sergeant as your boss, supervisor, teacher, spouse, or parent. It is never difficult to find something to criticize or ridicule; the opportunities are endless. If there is reprieve in a constant diet of criticism it is only that over time the barbs tend to lose their power and have less impact. Unfortunately, this can lead to escalation, turning up the volume on humiliation.

In between the two poles of affirming and disparaging is a middle ground of simply ignoring, not noticing or responding to what others do. This neutral gear neither affirms nor shames but rather pays no attention or at least remains silent. It is as though nothing deserves to be recognized. Although I regret some acts of sarcasm, I have mostly made my mistakes in this neutral zone. For a teacher or parent to say *nothing* either positive or negative can evoke anxiety and insecurity. One begins looking for hints and imagining what they might mean. A clinical supervisor once told me that I am a "projection magnet"—that when I remain silent people will tend to imagine that I am judging, disapproving, or criticizing. "You should have been a psychoanalyst," he said. "Clients would project onto you all of their negative parent material." Experience has proved him right. I had to learn to speak up more about what I appreciate in others and find better ways to listen than just remaining silent.

So what is affirming? It is paying attention to people's strengths, good efforts, contributions, and steps in the right direction, and not merely noticing but also acknowledging them. Your appreciation does no good if you keep it to yourself. Now, it's certainly possible to overdo this. Constant applause becomes meaningless. Far more common, though, is laxness in recognizing the good around us.

For better or worse, most change happens in small steps. It is what psychologist William James called the educational variety of change,[35] gradually learning bit by bit. We may fantasize that if we just confront people and make them see, then they will change suddenly and dramatically. There is in particular an odd belief, never supported by science, that if we can just make people feel *bad enough* about themselves, then they will change. If anything, the opposite is true: that when we feel unacceptable we are unable to change. Shame and humiliation are paralyzing. The strange paradox about human nature is that when you experience acceptance just as you are—whether from others (a parent, a teacher, a therapist), from God, even from yourself—then it becomes possible to change. I don't know why we are wired that way but it seems to be true.

So if change for better or worse most often happens a little bit at a time, then it matters to notice and encourage even small positive steps. Skillful teachers, parents, and counselors know this. I remember a client with a long history of alcohol problems who early in treatment told me, "I went two days without drinking this week." A moralistic gut response would be: "What? You mean you drank for five days?" Instead I managed to affirm this step in the right direction. "Wow! How did you do that? What was it like?" And before long he had put together four months of abstinence. Then one day he came in with his head hanging. "What's the matter?" I asked.

"I drank two days this week," he said, looking terribly ashamed. As it turned out he had gone to a graduation party where he had two drinks. The next day he had two more and then said to himself, "This is stupid. What am I doing this for?" and the following day he came in to see me mourning the loss of his sobriety.

"Well, that's one way to look at it," I said. "Now, as I recall you were drinking about ninety drinks a week when you first came in. You decided to quit and you've had four months with no alcohol. This week you had four drinks total. So that's roughly a 99 percent reduction over all that time, and you're clear that what you want to do from here on is get back on the wagon. That's great!" And in fact he went right back to being a nondrinker.

Perfection is a very high standard. It is what tends to doom New Year's resolutions. With the best of intentions you set a new rule like, "This year I'm not going to [*fill in the blank*]" For a while it goes well, but then comes the exception to the rule and the private recriminations. "Now I've done it." "I'm off my diet." "I blew it." "What's the point? I can't do it." Focusing on a single violation of an absolute rule can collapse perfectionism's house of cards. Better to focus on progress, on positive change, recognizing that imperfection is the human condition.[36]

Notice and affirm people's strengths rather than their shortcomings, their three steps forward rather than two steps back. It's what real friends do and for good reason. Affirming someone's good qualities, actions, and efforts tends to strengthen relationships. It also decreases the need to feel and be defensive, and increases openness to new information. In other words, affirmation is something we can do for each other that makes a real difference. Hold on to what is good! It is lovingkindness in action.

I end with a caution. When you become a consistently positive and affirming person for someone, you have a particular responsibility to rein in the negative. "You become responsible forever for what you have tamed," says the fox to Saint-Exupery's *Little Prince*.[37] Just as an occasional affirmation is surprisingly powerful when coming from a chronically negative person, so a sporadic zap from a reliably positive person can be especially painful. We have a responsibility not to wound those we love, and not to use this acquired power of negativity to control them.

Realizing

Present

As you proceed through a normal day, try consciously noticing things that are good, going right, done well, beautiful, or thoughtful, and comment on them. This may be especially important for the people you live with, work with, or see every day because it is easy to start taking them for granted (neutral gear) and not notice. Try out a beginner's mind as if you were experiencing these people and things for the first time and appreciating them. This can be particularly useful in a situation where you feel tempted to criticize. What might you find to affirm instead? What happens when you do?

Past

Think of people you have particularly admired or appreciated, who made a real difference in your life and are no longer around. They might be people you knew personally or only through appreciating their work, such as a musician, writer, or artist. Take time to write a short essay or story that describes what you appreciated about someone. Use the person's name and explain how he or she affected or inspired you. Be specific. Perhaps you will even write about several such people.

Future

Send a message of encouragement to people who could use it. Be specific about strengths and qualities you see in them and positive things they have done. Express your hope and encouragement for the future or in challenges they face. Perhaps include a small thoughtful gift that mirrors your affirmation.

12

Forgiveness

Forgiving   Resentful   Vengeful

A chilling massacre made international news in 2006. In Lancaster County, Pennsylvania, a heavily armed man entered a one-room Amish schoolhouse saying he could not forgive God for the death of his newborn daughter years before and was seeking revenge. He released the adults and all of the boys, then lined up the twelve- and thirteen-year-old girls on the floor, tied them up, and methodically shot them, murdering five before killing himself. The impact in the small community of West Nickel Mines was devastating, but what also appeared newsworthy in the days that followed was the response of the Amish whose children had been slain. Their immediate and sustained response was to forgive, shunning vengeance and comforting the killer's family. Some criticized such quick forgiveness for a person who had expressed no remorse and thus did not deserve pardon, but for the Amish it was what they needed to do and indeed no one else could do it for them.[38]

Forgiveness is a process that involves both head and heart. It is a choice to let go of your own feelings of anger, resentment, and entitlement; to release any lingering desire to return hurt for hurt, or at least to be open to reconciliation. No one but the offended party has the right or ability to forgive. Across the world's religions, forgiveness is commended if not commanded as a virtue, and the psychological and health benefits of forgiveness are well documented.[39] There is a much-quoted aphorism sometimes attributed to Alcoholics Anonymous that holding onto anger and resentment is like drinking poison and expecting the other person to die.

Here is another side of the affirming quality discussed in chapter 11 that holds onto what is good. The way of lovingkindness conversely does not hold onto what is hurtful. "Do not rejoice in evil."[40] Certainly do not celebrate inhumanity. Some cheered when seeing the nationally televised fireballs of the "shock and awe" bombing of Baghdad in 2003 that began the war in Iraq. As revenge for the 9/11 attacks it was misguided, but the broader point here is that the incineration of fellow members of the human family is cause for mourning, not celebration. It is debatable whether the destruction at New York or Baghdad, Hiroshima or Pearl Harbor was justifiable in order to achieve desired ends; whether we ought to *rejoice* in such slaughter is not, at least not through the eyes of lovingkindness.[41] There is a famous Midrash commentary on the Exodus story that is part of the Passover celebration.[42] As the sea closes over the Egyptian army pursuing the Israelites, the angels of heaven break into jubilant song, but God silences them: "My children are drowning and you are singing?" So first, don't celebrate, glamorize, or praise inhumanity. It is not how we are meant to be. Switch off the latest gossip or media feeding frenzy. There is too much else to do and celebrate! The challenging call of lovingkindness is to mourn with and for those who suffer, even when they are enemies.

True forgiveness lets go of the desire for revenge (a self-perpetuating reciprocal inhumanity) and also the neutral gear of lingering resentment. It is amazing what seemingly small slights or injustices people sometimes hold onto—cherishing, polishing, nurturing, and turning them over and over, sometimes for decades even within the small community of a neighborhood, congregation, workplace, or extended family. They rehearse the resentment until it poisons a relationship, sometimes even a whole group, and every thought of or contact with the offender yields a flash of pain or hatred. Such anger cannot endure over a long period without being constantly refueled. It is not good for anyone to hold onto such resentment.

There are greater offenses as well, those for which few would be surprised or blame a person for withholding forgiveness. The anger that blocks forgiveness can usually be justified, but justification is not the issue. What often stands in the way is that forgiveness gets confused with five other things that are not at all the same.

Five Things with which Forgiveness Gets Confused

1. Forgiveness is not *amnesia*. Forgiving and forgetting are two different acts. Forgiveness does not require forgetting, nor can one forgive that which has already been forgotten. Forgiveness is given with full memory of what happened. If anything, it is forgiveness that lets us finally lay to rest the bitter memories that we otherwise nurture for too long.

2. Forgiveness is not *acquittal*. Acquittal means finding a person to be guiltless, blameless, without responsibility for what happened. A person who is "not guilty" did no wrong or was not at fault, in which case forgiveness would not be needed. It is the very fact of the person's responsibility that requires forgiveness. To a person receiving forgiveness it may bring a freedom that feels like acquittal, perhaps even better than a legal exoneration after which doubts sometimes linger. Forgiveness is given with full knowledge that the person did it and was responsible. This also means that one need not deny responsibility in order to be forgiven.

3. Forgiveness is not *achieved*. It is not an award given only to those who have earned it or are most deserving. It is not earned, nor can it be. There are no hurdles over which a

person must jump before meriting forgiveness. If that were so it would be impossible to forgive someone with whom we have lost contact through death or otherwise. The choice to forgive is unwarranted. Not even remorse is required.

4. Forgiveness is not *approval*. To forgive another's action is not to condone the act. It does not require the forgiving person to say, "I think that what you did was really OK," or even, "I might have done the same thing in your situation" (although that is true more often than we might like to admit). Forgiveness is not needed from those who approve. It is needed and given precisely when we do not approve.

5. Finally, forgiveness is not *acquiescence*. It is not a license that reads, "Do whatever you like in the future, and it will be OK." To a woman who escaped being stoned to death Jesus said, "Neither do I condemn you. Go and sin no more."[43] It is not a suspension of values, an absence of rules or guidelines, nor is it permission to stay the same. To the contrary, forgiveness may inspire and enable change. Forgiveness is not acquiescence. It is a gift given with the knowledge that the future may or may not be different, but with a profound and active hope that it will.

Forgiveness, then, is none of these things. It is not amnesia or acquittal, not achieved, not approval or acquiescence. Rather, it is a choice to accept what is and move on. It is given without expectation of return. Forgiveness is an acceptance that may inspire change instead of waiting for it to happen. Rather than being a momentary once-and-for-all choice, forgiveness can be a process that occurs over time. It may be that some time must pass, and mind and heart mature a bit before the process can even begin.

The act of forgiveness does not require the other to be present. Indeed, the person you need to forgive may have been dead for twenty years. Neither does forgiveness require that you express it, for sometimes saying "I forgive you" could just make matters worse. For example, people who believe that they did nothing wrong may take offense at expressed forgiveness. It is really a choice that you make for your own physical, psychological, and spiritual health. If it also heals a relationship, all the better.

Emotional Forgiveness

Making a decision to forgive may be incomplete without emotional forgiveness, letting go of the hard feelings attached to a memory.[44] A choice to forgive can be made at any time, but negative emotions may linger and you're unlikely to make these disappear by willpower. It is lovingkindness, the very quality described in this book, that overcomes hatred. In private you can practice empathy (seeing and understanding things from the other's perspective), compassion, humility, hope, or acceptance—whatever affirms a humane attitude. You can also publicly express forgiveness (if doing so is unlikely to do harm), act on behalf of the other's well-being, or seek connection and reconciliation. Positive emotions and actions counteract the negative far better than does the mere passage of time.

Receiving Forgiveness

The familiar Lord's Prayer includes the injunction, "Forgive us our sins as we forgive those who sin against us." What does it mean? Is it calling down a curse upon ourselves that forgiveness of our shortcomings should be limited by our own capacity to forgive? No, that would be earning forgiveness. I think rather it is a kind of wiring diagram of the human psyche. It is a reminder that to the extent we fail to accept and forgive others we remain tormented ourselves. To be unforgiving is to be haunted by a sense of being unforgiven, unacceptable. To be forgiving and accepting of others is to inherit a sense of peacefulness. It's just part of how we are made.

So for the recipient, a circle of forgiveness is incomplete until it has been accepted. It is not easy to forgive. It is also not easy to accept forgiveness. It means first of all having to confront that for which we need forgiveness, to know that what we did was not OK, to accept responsibility for having done it, to know that we have not earned forgiveness, and to resolve to do better. That can evoke in us all manner of responses that block our acceptance of grace. We may turn the act over and over again in our minds, as if seeing it again would somehow absolve us. We struggle to explain why we did it, perhaps to rationalize or justify it, or maybe we connect it with other shortcomings of our past to form a pattern for which we can berate ourselves. There can be reluctance to enter into the contract of forgiveness. There is a temptation to ask, "Are you sure? Do you really forgive me? Don't you want me to suffer a little longer?"—bespeaking an underlying sense of "I don't deserve it" or "I don't forgive myself." The truth, of course, is that normally we have not earned it. Forgiveness is a choice for both giver and receiver, not time off for good behavior.

Do not cling to hurts or grievances. It is like clutching a burning coal. Do not refuse to forgive. It is like planting and fertilizing poisonous seedlings in your family garden. "I have decided to stick with love," said Dr. Martin Luther King Jr. "Hate is too great a burden to bear."

Realizing

Obstacles to Forgiveness

If you are holding onto a grudge, offense, or resentment, only you can release it. No one can forgive on your behalf. When it has been difficult for you to forgive, has it been because:

- Forgiving would require you to forget it?

- Forgiving would absolve the person of responsibility for what he or she did?

- The person did not earn or deserve your forgiveness?

- Forgiving would seem like saying that what the person did was OK?

- Forgiving would give the person permission not to change?

If so, review the discussion of these points earlier in this chapter and see if you can separate them from the releasing act of forgiveness.

Emotional Forgiveness

Where you harbor hard feelings toward someone, how might you counteract (act against) these negative emotions? Are there positive experiences you have shared with the person that you can revisit together or in memory? Can you find a connection of compassionate empathy? Is there a positive emotional experience (such as gratitude, hope, or acceptance) that you can call upon to release hard feelings? What positive actions (of generosity, empathy, affirmation, etc.) might you offer without expecting any gratitude or reciprocation?

13

Patience

Patient   Impatient   Intolerant

One year when I was in Amish country not far from where I grew up I had an opportunity to talk with a devout man who had come to town with a horse and plain black buggy. He was friendly and willing to chat, so I asked him why the Old Order Amish do not drive automobiles. I privately wondered whether it was some kind of superstition. "Well," he replied, "this is a healthy way of life that we choose and want to keep. It seems like when people start driving cars they get hurry-up disease."

Just yesterday a hardware store clerk said to me, "Sorry for your wait!" I had probably been standing there for ninety seconds while he helped the person in front of me. Some telephone customer service workers now seem to be trained to apologize every minute or two for any delays. Computers that once appeared to be lightning fast can now seem frustratingly slow. We are a culture trained to be impatient. We have hurry-up disease.

Some of this is technology-driven. On my first sabbatical leave in Norway the only communication options to and from the United States were airmail or very expensive telephone calls.

Except in emergencies we wrote letters and hoped for a reply within a couple of weeks. Seven years later the fax machine was available and people expected a response the next day. Seven years after that there was email and one could look for a reply the same day. Now we have cell phones and become impatient without an immediate answer.

Imagine a room full of people all of whom want their own needs to be met *right now*. (That is the everyday scenario in certain lines of service work.) At the extreme end, impatience becomes intolerance that feeds and is fed by a sense of entitlement. "I deserve for my needs to be met *first* and immediately. Get out of my way!"

A belief in entitlement is one of the walls of the prison of privilege (chapter 5). I have flown enough in my work to have earned certain airline privileges such as boarding planes early. In truth everyone on a plane arrives at the destination at the same time. Yet being accustomed to the privilege of early boarding, I can easily feel frustrated and put upon if I am flying on another airline where I board with group three or four. I feel entitled to board early and all of these other people are getting on before me! How very silly, and yet airlines have some of the most successful loyalty programs by offering such miniscule privileges.

Love is patient. It does not insist on immediate gratification or being first. It is willing to wait with expectation and curiosity, noticing and mindfully enjoying the present. In Thornton Wilder's play *Our Town* the deceased Emily revisits past moments in her life with new eyes of loving wonder, despairing that no one seems to realize and appreciate life while they are still living it.

Perhaps nowhere is the difference between patience and impatience more evident than in conversation. It is a rare gift to have someone listen to you with no agenda other than to understand who you are and what you mean (chapter 7). Far more common is a sense that the other person is not really listening or engaged, maybe looking around the room for someone or something more interesting. In ordinary conversation people may listen just long enough to know what they want to say next in response, even interrupting to say it: what the other person is saying is not really all that important; it merely provides an opportunity to share your own experience, wisdom, advice, and solutions.[45] At the intolerance (reverse gear) end of this character dimension people may be simply unwilling to listen and learn, convinced that others have nothing meaningful to offer them and that any experience or opinion different from their own is suspect.

One reflection of a listener's patience is how much talk time each person occupies. A good listener should not be doing most of the talking. Comfort with silence grows with patience. Ordinarily people may begin to feel awkward after a few seconds of silence in a conversation or meeting, as if someone should always be saying something. Some people, particularly introverts, just require longer to process what they are thinking or feeling, and allowing a bit of silence gives them an opportunity to do so.[46] As a therapist I find that what emerges after a span of silence is often far better than what I might have said or asked had I felt obliged to fill the gap.

I will keep this chapter short, lest you become impatient.

Realizing

Choose Patience

When you are in a store or other situation where there are several lines of people waiting, intentionally choose the longest line. It is a good antidote to the usual practice of trying to find the quickest line and then fretting when any other line moves faster.

Let go of thoughts that it is important for you to get there first when in fact it matters very little. Life is too short to hurry. It may be that the early bird gets the worm but, as they say, it is the second mouse who gets the cheese. Try experiencing traffic not as a competition sport but as a flowing river where things float along and merge naturally with the current.

Mindfulness

Do you have to wait a bit? Instead of fuming, pay close attention to the world around you. What do you see, hear, smell, and feel? Is there something in which you can notice beauty? What might you guess about the people around you? What do their faces tell you if you simply observe? Or use the waiting time to relax, breathe, meditate, or pray. Instead of feeling annoyed when a traffic light turns red, enjoy the opportunity to stop and take a moment to unwind.

Listening

When you have an opportunity for conversation, adopt the mind-set that your primary goal is just to understand what the other person is saying and experiencing (chapter 7). There is no need to be clever or a scintillating conversationalist. Patiently try to see the world through the other person's eyes, to understand what she or he means. At least for the time being, let go of the idea that you need to insert your own experience and wisdom. There is a certain peacefulness about this kind of listening. Wait and listen patiently for what this person and moment have to teach you.

14

Humility

Humble Immodest Arrogant

Perhaps the best reason for humility is that it is the truth. On the stage of human history we are all walk-on newcomers who will be exiting soon. Astronomers may have the best appreciation that on a universal scale within billions of galaxies we are infinitesimally tiny and momentary blips.

This is not at all to minimize the preciousness of life. To the contrary, it beckons us to savor and use well the life time that we have. Humility is not a false modesty that denies the truth or importance of your life; it is a matter of putting yourself into larger perspective.

I am grateful to have come across the writings of J. S. Neki, a psychiatrist who offered some telling observations about dependence and independence from the perspective of his native India.[47] He reflected in particular on the Western obsession with independence—that young people should shake off the shackles of dependence as soon as possible, and that it is a shameful thing if an adult ever must return to depending on others. The ideal within this viewpoint would be a life of total independence. How very strange! Better, he said, to allow children to enjoy the dependence of childhood without needing to fight against it, and to accept that it is normal to need more assistance and care as we grow older. If there are only dependent and independent people in the world, Neki asked, then who is dependable? The proper circle of interdependence is to grow from dependent to dependable and then, as needed, back toward dependence. We all rely on each other.

Immodesty involves an overblown sense of one's own importance that may be revealed in bragging, boasting, name-dropping, and such. Arrogance takes this one step further by demeaning the importance of others while assuming personal hierarchical status and privilege. It insists on the best seats in the house if not the throne. My own experience is that both immodesty and arrogance usually bespeak a needy pit of insecurity beneath.

Humility is first an inner experience, a knowing appreciation of our very limited place in time and space. To simulate humility without this inner perspective is false pretension. At heart, humility is unassuming, neither seeking notice or praise nor pretending to be what one is not. It is not arrogant or rude, dismissing others with labels or name-calling whether publicly or in the privacy of one's own thoughts. It does not linger on competitive comparisons that can leave you "vain and bitter; for always there will be greater and lesser persons than yourself."[48]

How is this inner humility manifested in daily life? Fundamentally it is to treat everyone with respect, which psychologist Carl Rogers called "unconditional positive regard."[49] Give your full attention when speaking with anyone and listen more than talking. If you are afforded or accustomed to privilege, participate in humble tasks and seek to serve more than being served. Defer if you are someone who expects deference. Approach the world with a curious beginner's mind rather than assuming that you already know.

I hasten to add that there are many for whom empowerment is needed more than any humbling. For those in need of building up, ego deflation is not the right recipe. It has been my experience that humility is more often a challenge for men than for women.

What is essential here is not putting oneself down but lifting others up and recognizing our common humanity.

There is a certain comfort and inner peace in the experience of humility. There is no need to compare or prove your importance because the truth is that everyone has inherent worth and deserves respect. There is no "king of the hill" anxiety about hanging onto status, which is an ephemeral illusion. It is enough to rest in your worthy true self, the very essence of which is lovingkindness.

Realizing

Awe

Awe is our human experience of wonder at being in the presence of something far greater than ourselves. When have you experienced awe? For me it is often in nature: being under a moonless sky filled with stars or standing on the rim of the Grand Canyon or a vast ocean. For one man I met it was holding in his hand an arrowhead carefully crafted from bone thousands of years ago. The astonishing complexity of the human body is reason enough for awe. What inspires in you that kind of wonderment at—and yet perhaps connectedness with—what is far beyond you in time, space, and consciousness? Write about an experience of awe from your own life. Then share it with a friend and ask him or her to relate another experience of awe.

Unassuming

The idea of *practicing* humility suggests pretension because true modesty arises from within. Nevertheless, there come moments of choice between status or humility, boasting or modesty. In such situations what does it mean not to "assume"? If you might ordinarily occupy an upper position (for example, authority, power, status, or wisdom), try instead deferring with curiosity to others' wisdom and experience. See what happens.

15

Gratitude

Grateful   Unappreciative   Entitled

Gratitude is another aspect of lovingkindness that is admired across cultures and honored among world religions. The attitude underlying gratitude is one of appreciation that extends even to small things. As with affirming (chapter 11), gratitude is first of all noticing, paying attention to what is good. What is there to be thankful for in your life, even at this very moment? As I write this on an airplane I notice some simple pleasures: the clever and convenient design of my favorite type of pen and the soft but firm and comfortable seat that supports me. I reflect on the countless people living and dead who have been kind and important to me. I am aware of the joy of bodily life itself despite some aches and pains of aging, and I give thanks for what doesn't hurt and what I am able to do. I think with curious anticipation of the travel on which I am embarking and what new experiences it will bring. Past, present, and future are all fertile fields in harvesting reasons for gratitude.

But don't merely notice. Paying attention is a first step, but savor, celebrate, appreciate! Take time to enjoy the present, to remember past joys and kindnesses, to envision future possibilities.

How easy it is to revisit hurts and resentments, turning them over and over in our minds and thus strengthening their grip on us. Choose instead to obsess about blessings!

These two steps—first noticing and then appreciating—are private experiences. You can do them without anyone else being present. But there is something better still in shared experience, and a third step is acknowledging your gratitude, expressing your thanks. It can be as simple as saying "thank you!" or as profound as a heartfelt voicing of all you are grateful for. Thanksgiving is also a common form of prayer. Shared gratitude doesn't have to be about anything the other person did. It can be about a shared experience. Look at that wonderful sunset! Such a fine meal! What an amazing performance!

To be unappreciative is the neutral gear on this character dimension: when the kindness of others goes unnoticed or unacknowledged. "Taking for granted" is another way to describe ingratitude. In ongoing relationships where lovingkindness has been the norm it is easy to get careless about noticing and appreciating acts of kindness. In relationships where someone is expected and paid to be courteous it might seem unnecessary to express thanks. It is the absence of a grateful response that characterizes this middle ground. Then there is the far end of the spectrum where the response to kindness is entitlement or abuse. This is beyond a lack of appreciation; kindness is not only disregarded but is met with a disdainful, critical, or otherwise hurtful response. There is no apparent felt need for civility. These are the least favorite customers of those in service professions.

To cultivate gratitude, to consciously practice thankfulness, is a remedy for creeping entitlement that is one of the walls of the prison of privilege (chapter 5). Gratitude is also just common courtesy (though sometimes not so common).

Realizing

Privately

Gratitude can become a daily practice. The old adage is to count your blessings. Some choose a particular time of day to reflect on thankfulness in meditation or prayer. Some express their gratitude in a journal, which also allows you to return and review what you have written earlier. Combining with a patience exercise you could use moments of waiting, like at a traffic light or in a line, to celebrate that for which you are thankful or just to savor the beauty of the moment. You can also revisit the *Dayenu* exercise from chapter 9.

Expressing Stored-Up Gratitude

Think of someone who made a real positive difference in your life, who took time and care as your teacher, coach, coworker, or friend—someone who is still living but perhaps you haven't seen for a while. Take time to write a message of thanks to them, maybe a handwritten letter, expressing your gratitude for them as a person, for what they did and how they did it, and for the difference it has made in your life. Then send it.

16

Helpfulness

Helpful Unhelpful Obstructive

Helpfulness is a companion virtue of gratitude. To "pay it forward" is to offer unearned help and generosity without expecting anything in return. It may be motivated by gratitude for help received from others along the way, a passing along of past generosity in your own life. It reflects concern beyond yourself for the well-being of others. Within the program of Alcoholics Anonymous, the final of the twelve steps involves carrying the message to others. Communities and cultures vary widely in this sense of interdependence and collective responsibility for each other. Sometimes a crisis such as a natural disaster evokes inspiring levels of altruistic cooperation.

Helpfulness involves doing more than just what is required. It is seeing something that needs to be done and doing it without being asked. It's what valued team members, employees, and family members do. As with the other dimensions of lovingkindness, people generally honor helpfulness as an admirable aspect of character. It promotes the common good, sometimes at cost or inconvenience to oneself. More generally, altruistic service to others (such as hospitality to strangers) is a value shared across world religions. Such helpfulness extends outside one's own social circle, from simple courtesy to assisting those in need. Lovingkindness particularly seeks to help the vulnerable and marginalized. As mentioned in chapter 6, "to help other people at all times" has been part of the law and promises of both Girl and Boy Scouts for more than a century.

At the reverse end of the spectrum are people who seem to thrive on thwarting and frustrating others. This can be done in a dominating or a passive-aggressive manner. They may find fault with most any idea other than their own and specialize in explaining why changes won't work. In between is the neutral zone of plain unhelpfulness, neither impeding nor aiding.

Being helpful can be done for practical reasons. If I do things that benefit those around me, then they will help me when I need it. If I am willing to collaborate and make some compromise, then I can anticipate cooperation when I try to get something else done. If I contribute, then I get something of value in return. This is the "social contract" of a collective group or society, literally a "commonwealth."

Social contracts do serve the well-being of group members, but the call of lovingkindness is larger than this: to recognize our common connectedness with all of humankind or with all of life. The quantum changers described in chapter 1 saw this in a sudden insight or epiphany that transformed their lives. Acting on behalf of people outside your usual comfort zone offers the opportunity to enrich your breadth of human experience. How easily we become segregated by age, race, or social class, associating only with people similar to ourselves!

I reiterate a caution here that it is important to have a solid spiritual foundation yourself if you choose to spend significant time in serving others. Mindfulness meditation or contemplative prayer can offer this quiet center, as can lovingkindness meditations (see endnotes 17–19). Without such a solid center, helping may be done in service to your own ego ("Look what a good person I am!") and can lead to burnout or compassion fatigue. My focus in this book is on realizing lovingkindness, expressing it in action, but I do not mean to understate the importance of a spiritual or other centering practice. Quakers, Mennonites, and Buddhists have particularly embodied this balance between the inner journey and active service to others.

A further caution is that being helpful requires good listening to understand the person's perspective and needs (see chapter 7). Without taking the time to listen well there's a danger of imposing your own values and interpretation, particularly with people who are quite different from you. As a result, what you intend as helpful may not be what the person needs, or still worse may be harmful.

Realizing

With Charity toward All

With whom do you spend most of your time? Many people live in a kind of apartheid isolation, associating primarily or exclusively with others like themselves. It may require intentional steps to spend time with people who are quite different from yourself economically, culturally, or in age or education. This often includes moving outside your everyday comfort zone. What are your own values about relating to or helping people who are different from yourself? What groups of people do you almost never see? Where and how might you come into contact with and get to know them? How might you practice lovingkindness toward them? Choose a particular person whom you ordinarily do not see or speak with. Take time to have a real conversation, primarily listening. Notice your responses when stepping outside your familiar comfort zone.

Gifts

What skills, talents, or other gifts do you have that you might use in service to others? What are you particularly good at? What do you enjoy doing? Write down a list, and don't be shy about it. Who might benefit from this skill and experience of yours? Where might you volunteer some time to use your skills? Contact one place just to ask how volunteers are able to help there.

Serving

What are your own motivations for serving or helping others? What keeps you going? What, if anything, do you expect from them in return? Is it important that the people you help show gratitude? The next time you are trying to be helpful pay attention to how the person or people respond, and to your own thoughts and feelings as you interact.

17

Yielding

Yielding   Unyielding   Dominating

My psychologist colleague Carl Thoresen at Stanford University was working with patients (mostly men) in the San Francisco Bay area who had survived a heart attack and didn't want to have another one. They were all from the same large workplace and many fit the "type A" profile, a heart-attack-prone personality that is hard-driving, angry, competitive, and time-pressured. Every workday they drove from home to work and back in the notorious traffic of the Bayshore Freeway, a commute of an hour or so at most busy times. They were usually dodging and cursing slower drivers, cutting in and out, changing lanes while scanning for any possible opening that might allow them to get a little ahead.

Carl gave them behavioral assignments that were appealing in the first week and appalling in the second. For five work days they were to drive as usual at the same time of day trying to get from home to work as quickly as possible, recording their door-to-door time each way. They loved this assignment. When they arrived at work a nurse was waiting in a special parking area to take their heart rate and blood pressure and administer a short stress scale. Then during the second week Carl instructed them to get in the right-hand (slowest) freeway lane and stay there, again recording their driving time and checking in with the nurse when they arrived at work. The Bayshore Freeway had many entrance lanes whereby incoming drivers must merge left into ongoing traffic. This meant that driving in the right lane required yielding regularly to entering vehicles, allowing them to merge. They hated this assignment and were vehement that it would take far longer and they would arrive much more frustrated and stressed by the dangerous merging.

To the drivers' amazement the average door-to-door time difference between the fast and slow weeks was 101 seconds, and all of them had significantly lower heart rate, blood pressure, and stress levels in week two. This was just one component of a complex behavior-change intervention, but at the end of the first year the death rate from another heart attack was significantly lowered in the treatment group.[50]

To give way, to negotiate and compromise can be seen in politics as weakness. It is also generally how to get things done in business, government, institutions, and in life. A win/lose perspective is understandable in competition sports but it is a recipe for conflict and gridlock in most social interactions.

The character dimension here stretches from yielding at the forward end, unyielding in the neutral position, and dominating at the far end. Yield to someone in traffic and you often get a wave of thanks, at least from the person in front of you. We rather universally recognize it as a voluntary act of kindness. When two vehicles are approaching the same parking space, dominating (zooming in to claim it) versus yielding will have very different emotional consequences for both drivers.

This character dimension also gets reflected in styles of leadership. Unyielding leaders, though not necessarily coercive, tend not to value differing opinions or change their minds in response to others' concerns. Authoritarian leaders—a dominating style—lord it over others, using power to enforce their own will and values. At the opposite end are servant leaders who regard themselves as working for and with others. They perceive that the further up they go in a hierarchy, the more people they serve. They listen well, taking into account varied opinions and needs. Their management style tends to be collaborative and transparent, a shared leadership approach.

Richard Rohr has contrasted the differing tasks of the first and second halves of life.[51] The first half tends to be about taking control and establishing a separate identity, family, and career. The tasks of the second half are much more about letting go, accepting, turning over, and releasing. Trying to continue controlling everything is not a happy strategy for launching your children, growing older, empowering the next generation, or retiring. Yet our society offers few models for how to live the second half of life or even awareness that there is one. It is never too early to begin practicing this character strength of voluntary yielding.

Of course, there is no justice when yielding is all one-sided. Compromise (literally to promise together) is about making reasonable allowance for each other while ensuring that both parties' needs are being met. Instead of a win/lose contest, lovingkindness seeks a balance in meeting the needs and concerns of all involved.

Underlying this dimension of lovingkindness is an acceptance that we all get to make our own choices. As much as we might sometimes wish to make other people's choices for them, we cannot do that. In fact, there is a predictable counter-reaction to any perceived loss of freedom.[52] People resent and resist coercive control, and when a previously available option is threatened it tends to become all the more desirable. This is one reason why punishment is notoriously ineffective in overcoming bad habits and addictions. If suffering cured addiction there wouldn't be any.

Human beings are both autonomous and interconnected—a seeming paradox, but I find that many deep truths are paradoxical. Lovingkindness honors others' autonomy while also recognizing and embracing our interrelatedness.

Realizing

Voluntary Yielding

Look for small opportunities to practice the generosity of yielding. Are you going to the post office, bank, or no-appointment haircut shop where the earliest person through the door gets in line first? Hold the door for someone else, allowing them to go before you. Is there someone behind you in the checkout line who has only a few items? Offer the opportunity to check out first. Where in your daily life could you find such opportunities to practice voluntary yielding?

Negotiating

The term "negotiation" conjures up business dealings, but in fact we are constantly negotiating in everyday life. There is a dance of give and take whenever we ask someone to do something, when we walk down a crowded street, when we divide up tasks within a family or group. In navigating life we make allowances for each other. The next time you are faced with a disagreement or potential conflict, make it a priority to first understand clearly the other person's perspective and concerns (see chapter 7). The goal is not to win a disagreement or conflict, but to come to a mutual understanding and win/win agreement. That requires good listening as well as some yielding.

18

Integrity: Loving Kindness

An ideal attribute of lovingkindness (and of the twelve dimensions discussed in the preceding chapters) is that it is consistent (steadfast, reliable, enduring, dependable). It is not present at some times and absent at others. It is not offered to a favored few and withheld from others. Integrity is about living with that kind of consistency. Yet such integrity is not a starting point; it is a distant horizon toward which we move.

Something vital to know about virtues such as lovingkindness is that you do not need to wait for them to fully flower inside you before you begin living them. Indeed, you would wait forever because like musical virtuosity, virtues develop by being practiced. Love that is felt but never expressed or acted upon is not yet real. Love is realized in the doing, in the day-to-day process of living it out. Lovingkindness does not wait for some inner level of tide before flowing outward. It becomes real only when enacted. What good is a sympathetic feeling for hungry people if we do nothing to feed them?[53] Lovingkindness is something that you practice, and in the very doing over time it changes you.

In Isaac Bashevis Singer's short story "A Piece of Advice,"[54] a renowned rabbi offers counsel that transforms a chronically angry man into a good-natured fellow. "The main thing is to act, not to ponder . . . If you are not happy, act the happy man. Happiness will come later. So also with faith. If you are in despair, act as though you believed. Faith will come afterwards." Shakespeare's Hamlet offers similar advice: "Assume a virtue if you have it not . . . for use can almost change the stamp of nature."

I think, in fact, that practice actually can (not just almost) change our nature. It is in this way that one grows into lovingkindness. Each small compassionate act adds a tiny weight to the mass of your compassion, just as surely as withholding compassion of which you are capable numbs and subtracts from it. Here is the art of "living as if," of practicing a new way of being until it becomes second nature.

A modern confusion here is that the word *love* can mean so many different things. Ancient Greek contained at least four different words, all of which get translated as *love* in English.[55] It is *agape* that is selfless lovingkindness, and it can be confused with the other three. There is affection that one feels for family or dear friends (*philia*) and romantic erotic attraction (*eros*). There is also sentimental attachment as in "I *love* that valley" (*storge*). We are not called to have affectionate, sentimental, or romantic feelings toward strangers, clients, or those who harm us. In one way, the ancient exhortation to love our enemies or strangers is much simpler than that, and in another sense it is more difficult. It is simpler because it is usually easier to decide to *do* something than to *feel* something. You can choose your actions more readily than your feelings, although both are subject to self-control. Yet loving enemies is more difficult because the particular actions involved may run counter to your practiced nature, to current feelings, impulses, and comforts. It requires a kind of override, an overruling of what might at first seem the natural and justified response.

The path of lovingkindness is not an easy one. Ordinarily, people are more likely to continue an action that is rewarded or personally gratifying. Here is another paradox. In Jewish and Christian understanding as well as other world religions, lovingkindness is recognized particularly when we act on behalf of others without any hope or expectation of personal gain, and without regard for the other's merit. Acts of lovingkindness are particularly noble when they are unwarranted.

There is a special power to acts of lovingkindness that are unmerited, more so than when the kindness is what anyone else might do in the same situation. They can sometimes have an unexpected effect on others, whether it be the beneficiary of the act or a witness to it. Lovingkindness can have the power to inspire or move, shame or open, reconcile, transform, strengthen, or evoke repentance. The effect may be evident in a dramatic moment of turnabout, but much more often it is in a gradual shift, a subtle softening, the seeing of a new possibility, a willingness to consider.

At the outset of this book I said that lovingkindness is not only something that we *can* do, but in a larger sense it is what we *must* do. That is not literally true. We don't have to do it. We do have an inescapable choice. In Judeo-Christian tradition the thought itself does not make it so, even for God. It must be spoken or otherwise enacted into being. In eating of the forbidden fruit from the tree of the knowledge of good and evil, humankind became no longer innocent in action. We can choose, form an intention, and then either follow through with it or not.

Religious traditions differ on whether loving is our first nature, but in all of them it is a moral and honorable choice that we can make. They differ on the fundamental nature of deity and of humankind. For reasons explained earlier, I choose to affirm that lovingkindness is our fundamental human nature, that it is what we are meant to do and be. Again, it is not what we necessarily have to be. It is not mandated or predestined. The awesome and sobering truth is that we can choose between humanity and inhumanity, between love and its opposites. As I also said in the preface, inhumanity's opposite—that which brings light into darkness—is not passivity. The opposite of inhumanity is lovingkindness.

What do I mean, then, by saying that lovingkindness is what we *must* do? Not that we have no other choice, for the truth is that we do. Neither can we escape the choice. We each live our daily lives contributing some balance of inhumanity, neutrality, and lovingkindness, moving away from or toward our *telos*, our intended fully mature state. What I mean is that it is of ultimate importance how we choose if we are to survive and mature as humankind.

Whatever you may believe about afterlife—personally I entrust that to God—we leave our footprint in this life in a net balance of lovingkindness: our net worth, if you will. The collective life of the human race is shaped by choices to love or not. Inhumanity tends to breed more inhumanity across time until someone decides that *it stops here, with me.* Lovingkindness is similarly contagious. It inspires more of the same in ourselves and in others. Lovingkindness is perhaps the one good and reliable thing that we can pass across time, across death, across generations. It comes down to being a loving presence in the world, a way of being.

Because lovingkindness grows and multiplies, its practice changes us. We practice the constant, renewed intention and decision to love until lovingkindness becomes second nature (or is it actually a return to our first nature as human-kind?). What might once have required a willful, effortful, even grudging choice becomes easier, more natural. Perfection, in the sense of errorless performance, is beyond our human grasp. In a *telos* sense, however, the acorn is gradually perfected into the mighty oak, knots and all. In the end, we come to love kindness itself, and for itself. It becomes pleasing simply to love, without regard to return. Then is lovingkindness complete and your true nature realized.

Endnotes

1. William R. Miller and Janet C'de Baca, *Quantum Change: When Epiphanies and Sudden Insights Transform Ordinary Lives* (New York: Guilford, 2001); William R. Miller and Janet C'de Baca, "Quantum Change: Toward a Psychology of Transformation," in *Can Personality Change?*, edited by Todd F. Heatherton and Joel Lee Weinberger (Washington, DC: American Psychological Association, 1994), 253–80; Janet C'de Baca and William R. Miller, "Quantum Change: Sudden Transformation in the Tradition of James's *Varieties*," *Streams of William James* 5 (2003) 12–15; William R. Miller, "The Phenomenon of Quantum Change," *Journal of Clinical Psychology: In Session* 60 (2004) 453–60.

2. Paul Tillich, "You Are Accepted," in *The Shaking of the Foundations* (New York: Scribner, 1948), 162.

3. Janet C'de Baca and Paula Wilbourne, "Quantum Change: Ten Years Later," *Journal of Clinical Psychology* 60 (2004) 531–41.

4. C. S. Lewis, *The Abolition of Man* (Oxford: Oxford University Press, 1944).

5. https://www.charterforcompassion.org/charter; Karen Armstrong, *Twelve Steps to a Compassionate Life* (New York: Knopf, 2010).

6. John A. Bargh and Tanya L. Chartrand, "The Unbearable Automaticity of Being," *American Psychologist* 54 (1999) 462–79; John A. Bargh and Melissa J. Ferguson, "Beyond Behaviorism: On the Automaticity of Higher Mental Processes," *Psychological Bulletin* 126 (2000) 925–45.

7. Viktor E. Frankl, *Man's Search for Meaning* (Boston: Beacon, 2006).

8. Philip J. Newell, *Listening for the Heartbeat of God: A Celtic Spirituality.* (Mahwah, NJ: Paulist, 1997).

9. Abraham H. Maslow, *Motivation and Personality*, 2nd ed. (New York: Harper & Row, 1970); Carl R. Rogers, "The Nature of Man," in *The Nature of Man in Theological and Psychological Perspective,* edited by Simon Doniger (New York: Harper, 1962), 91–96.

10. Matt 5:48.

11. William R. Miller, *Living As If: Your Road, Your Life.* (Carson City, NV: Change Companies, 2008).

12. Matt 25:42–43.

13. Luke 6:32–34.

14. Mark 12:31; Matt 22:39, quoting Lev 19:18.

15. Matt 5:44. It is this teaching that Jesus concludes with the admonition to "be perfect [*telos*, complete, mature] even as God is perfect" (Matt 5:48).

16. 1 Cor 13.

17. Richard Rohr, *Dancing Standing Still: Healing the World from a Place of Prayer* (New York: Paulist, 2014); Thomas Keating, *Intimacy with God: An Introduction to Centering Prayer,* 3rd ed. (New York: Crossroad, 2009); Dalai Lama, *How to Practice: The Way to a Meaningful Life,* translated and edited by Jeffrey Hopkins (New York: Pocket Books, 2002).

18. Herbert Benson and Miriam Z. Klipper, *The Relaxation Response* (New York: HarperTorch, 2000); Jon Kabat-Zinn, *Mindfulness for Beginners: Reclaiming the Present Moment and Your Life* (Boulder, CO: Sounds True, 2012).

19. Sharon Salzberg, *Lovingkindness: The Revolutionary Art of Happiness* (Boston: Shambhala, 1995).

20. Angelina Isabella Mellentin et al., "Seeing Enemies? A Systematic Review of Anger Bias in the Perception of Facial Expressions among Anger-Prone and Aggressive Populations," *Aggression and Violent Behavior* 25 (2015) 373–83.

21. Richard Wilkinson and Kate Pickett, *The Spirit Level: Why Greater Equality Makes Societies Stronger* (New York: Bloomsbury, 2010).

22. Scott C. Miller, *Until It's Gone: Ending Poverty in Our Nation in Our Lifetime* (Highlands, TX: Aha! Process, 2008).

23. Joan K. Jackson, "The Adjustment of the Family to the Crisis of Alcoholism," *Quarterly Journal of Studies on Alcohol* 15 (1954) 562–86.

24. Thomas Gordon, *Parent Effectiveness Training: The No-Lose Program for Raising Responsible Children* (New York: Wyden, 1970).

25. Henri J. M. Nouwen, *In Memoriam* (Notre Dame, IN: Ave Maria, 2005).

26. Phil 4:11–12 (NIV).

27. Richard Rohr, *Simplicity: The Art of Living*, translated by Peter Heinneg, rev. ed. (New York: Crossroad, 2003); Bill Hybels, *Simplify: Ten Practices to Unclutter Your Soul* (Carol Stream, IL: Tyndale, 2015).

28. Comedian George Carlin offered an iconic skit on this topic in his 1981 recording, *A Place for My Stuff*.

29. Richard Rohr and Andreas Ebert, *Discovering the Enneagram: An Ancient Tool for a New Spiritual Journey*, translated by Peter Heinegg (New York: Crossroad, 1991).

30. Roy F. Baumeister, Todd F. Heatherton, and Dianne M. Tice, *Losing Control: How and Why People Fail at Self-Regulation* (New York: Academic Press, 1994).

31. Wayne Muller, *Sabbath: Finding Rest, Renewal, and Delight in Our Busy Lives* (New York: Bantam, 2000).

32. George J. Leake and Albert S. King, "Effect of Counselor Expectations on Alcoholic Recovery," *Alcohol Health and Research World* 1 (1977) 16–22.

33. William R. Miller, *Living As If: How Positive Faith can Change Your Life* (Philadelphia: Westminster Press, 1985).

34. I thank my friend and colleague Dr. Carolina Yahne for this useful exercise.

35. William James, *The Varieties of Religious Experience* (New York: Longmans, 1902).

36. A marvelous book full of wise stories on this subject is Ernest Kurtz and Katherine Ketcham, *The Spirituality of Imperfection: Storytelling and the Journey to Wholeness* (New York: Bantam, 1992).

37. Antoine de Saint-Exupéry, *The Little Prince*, translated by Katherine Woods (New York: Harcourt, 1943).

38. John L. Ruth, *Forgiveness: A Legacy of the West Nickel Mines Amish School* (Scottsdale, PA: Herald, 2007).

39. Everett L. Worthington et al., "Forgiveness, Health, and Well-Being: A Review of Evidence for Emotional Versus Decisional Forgiveness, Dispositional Forgiveness, and Reduced Unforgiveness," *Journal of Behavioral Medicine* 30 (2007) 291–302.

40. 1 Cor 13:6.

41. Mark Twain penned a drama called *The War Prayer* that he refused to publish before his death. In it a minister prays at a worship service for the safety and success of soldiers going off to war. The prayer is answered by the visit of a messenger "from the Throne" who vividly describes the suffering that fulfillment of the prayer would necessarily inflict on the men, women, and children of the other side, and then asks whether the congregation truly wants this.

42. Talmud, Meg. 10b.

43. John 8:11.

44. Everett L. Worthington, *Forgiving and Reconciling: Bridges to Wholeness and Hope* (Downers Grove, IL: InterVarsity, 2003).

45. Thomas Gordon's *Effectiveness Training* books explain in clear, everyday language how real "active" listening differs from the "roadblock" responses that we often make, even when trying to be helpful.

46. Susan Cain, *Quiet: The Power of Introverts in a World that Can't Stop Talking* (New York: Random House, 2013).

47. J. S. Neki, "An Examination of the Cultural Relativism of Dependence as a Dynamic of Social and Therapeutic Relationships. I. Socio-developmental," *British Journal of Medical Psychology* 49 (1976) 1–10; J. S. Neki, "An Examination of the Cultural Relativism of Dependence as a Dynamic of Social and Therapeutic Relationships. II. Therapeutic," *British Journal of Medical Psychology* 49 (1976) 11–22.

48. Max Ehrmann, *Desiderata: A Poem for a Way of Life* (New York: Crown, 1995).

49. Carl R. Rogers, *A Way of Being* (Boston: Houghton Mifflin, 1980).

50. M. Friedman et al., "Feasibility of Altering Type A Behavior Pattern After Myocardial Infarction: Recurrent Coronary Prevention Project Study: Methods, Baseline Results, and Preliminary Findings," *Circulation* 66 (1982) 83–92.

51. Richard Rohr, *Falling Upward: A Spirituality for the Two Halves of Life* (San Francisco: Jossey-Bass, 2011).

52. Sharon S. Brehm and Jack W. Brehm, *Psychological Reactance: A Theory of Freedom and Control* (New York: Academic Press, 1981).

53. Jas 2:14–17.

54. In Isaac Bashevis Singer, *The Spinoza of Market Street* (New York: Farrar, Straus and Giroux, 1979).

55. C. S. Lewis, *The Four Loves* (New York: Harcourt Brace, 1960).